WHAT PEOPLE ARE SA

THE RUSH HOUR ...

The Rush Hour Shaman is a gem of a book that is filled with tools to teach us how to reconnect with Nature, the helping spirits guiding us, and own inner healer. Jan Gale presents innovative ceremonies to help integrate our spiritual work into our daily lives. She is a wonderful writer, shamanic healer and teacher. This book is important for all of us who need inspiration in how to bring beauty, power, and healing into our modern day world. **Sandra Ingerman**, MA, author of *Soul Retrieval* and *The Shaman's Toolkit*

Jan takes us on a journey to inner strength using a straight-forward, innovative and well thought-out process. Her book acts like a navigation system guiding us to our highest potential. Jan shares with us ways to allow us to take time out of each busy day to focus on ourselves, and be grounded. We are given permission and directions to 'reduce our speed' and erect 'under construction' signs in order to create spiritual strength. More and more people are living in urban areas, so this timely book gives us the tools to stay connected with nature in unique ways, and look for the guidance we need to be fulfilled. **Maggie Schofield**, Executive Director, The Calgary Downtown Association

The Rush Hour Shaman

Shamanic Practices for Urban Living

The Rush Hour Shaman

Shamanic Practices for Urban Living

Janet Elizabeth Gale

Winchester, UK
Washington, USA

First published by Moon Books, 2014
Moon Books is an imprint of John Hunt Publishing Ltd., Laurel House, Station Approach,
Alresford, Hants, SO24 9JH, UK
office1@jhpbooks.net
www.johnhuntpublishing.com
www.moon-books.net

For distributor details and how to order please visit the 'Ordering' section on our website.

Text copyright: Janet Elizabeth Gale 2013

ISBN: 978 1 78279 466 0

A CIP catalogue record for this book is available from the British Library.

Design: Lee Nash

Printed and bound in the USA by Edwards Brothers Malloy

We operate a distinctive and ethical publishing philosophy in all
areas of our business, from our global network of authors to
production and worldwide distribution.

CONTENTS

Illustration

The Rush Hour Shaman. Pen and Ink by Roland Rollinmud, 2013, Morley, Alberta, Canada

Dedicated to all the Helping Spirits,
who support me in my life.

Introduction

Shamans from throughout history must be shaking their heads in frustration, watching us from their ethereal vantage points. We are no longer living in a world that relies on their skills for tracking game to feed the tribe, nor do we seem to require their amazing healing techniques. We don't seem to be very interested in exploring our planet, or the rich cultural diversity of others who live on it, unless it is a mindless trip to an exotic beach vacation in far away climes. We are far more interested in buying the latest techno toy or shaving ten minutes off the commute to work, than we are about looking at what our lives would be like if we were truly connected to our highest selves.

A significant number of us are glued to the TV, watching the sad life of an addicted celebrity or a horrific environmental tragedy. Not once do we turn the mirror around to look at ourselves. We stress about the stranger who cuts us off in rush hour, never considering why this might have happened. How much we could learn about our own lives if we took as much time to observe what was happening for us emotionally or spiritually as we spend observing what is going on outside of ourselves.

Instead, we are busy comparing our lives to another's. We rarely feel what is going on in our bodies as we self-judge, blame, feel inferior or superior, or exert power and control over another. We are leading busy and distracting lives. We rarely honor the precious spiritual self, are often disconnected from our intuition. We are seldom present. We are often so disconnected from our sixth sense that if we have a moment of spiritual authenticity, we might not even recognize it.

Through the loving intentions of a few spiritual leaders, there is an awakening of a newer consciousness. Gifted and heartfelt celebrities such as Louise Hay, Gary Zukav and Oprah have allowed a number of us to recognize that we have been sleeping.

We have been numbed to the wisdom of our physical bodies, as we robotically drive the same road into the office, not even noticing the person in the next vehicle, other than to curse them if they get ahead of us in line. As we wake up, we are realizing that we have lost touch with Mother Earth, and the wisdom that she holds. As we begin to feel and acknowledge the importance of our being, we are noticing that our emotions allow us to feel things in our bodies, and these sensations mean something. We are beginning to open to the possibilities that we are much more than our physical bodies and that our physical bodies are not the container of our souls, but that we are souls that exist in this lifetime as human physical forms to experience feelings and emotions.

There is an awakening occurring. Self help books leap off the shelves into shopping baskets. People flock to have energy work done on them. They understand that even though a practitioner doesn't have his hands on their body, they can receive healing. Studies have been done on the power of positive thinking and prayer. Scientists are backing up the hypotheses. Cameras and software have been developed to read our personal energy fields.

We are starting to remember that we are spiritual beings, and have sought the spiritual path in a variety of ways.

One of the issues that I have heard a lot about in my own healing practice has been that clients and friends have no problem being "spiritual" while attending a workshop or during a healing session, but it seems that they are working without a net out in the "real world". These people feel very connected to the earth and to the other participants at a workshop while they are relaxing in the redwoods, or gazing out into the ocean, but as soon as they come to the first stop light on their first day back to work, all the bliss has dissipated.

It is my intention to offer tools to assist you in integrating what you may have learned in a workshop or in a healing session. I hope to offer you some guidance into how to reconnect with nature and learn about the healer within you. These tools may offer support for reminding you daily of your wholeness and honor the beautiful energetic being that you are. The methods that are contained in this book may help you in realizing your potential, guiding you through life's problems and issues, and connecting you with others who are making their best efforts to do the same.

As we reach out toward our magnificent potential, raise our vibrational energy, and heal ourselves, we become powerful agents for effecting positive change on this planet!

Chapter One

Intention and the Pathway to Peace – or – Which Lane Merges Onto the Freeway?

If you have done any spiritual work, read a book recently, or even overheard a conversation at a coffee shop, you have probably heard that our thoughts and words have energy, and intention is "everything".

As a shamanic practitioner and energy healer, I can tell you that those statements are true. What is even more important to me, however, is that we should be aware of the emotional origin of our intention, and how the agenda of this emotion might be shaping our world.

Our personality has been formed through our years living on this Earth School. We have been conditioned by our upbringing, and the circumstances we have created through this upbringing have resulted in our having many unhealthy reactions in our personal classrooms here. When I went to school, we were never taught that we could make choices about how we could create our lives, only to do as we were told. Many years later, I have become very aware that I was creating my reality from fearful parts of my personality; reinforcing the belief I held that choices were not available to me. I was not responsible for my life by holding onto this belief. My experience was quite typical, as a person who thought life happened *to* me, not *for* me or *by* me.

With this limiting belief I held, it was very easy for me to be a victim to circumstance. Although very successful academically in school, I really never felt socially accepted. I lived in perpetually increasing fear that I was less than others physically and intellectually. With this thought having so much power over me, I was creating distance and separation from the very people that I thought I wanted to be close to. I pushed them away before they could reject me for being different. I fed that particular fear for much of my life, and it is something that I still challenge, even though I am more aware of the thought's existence and how it might take control of my actions or words when it is active in me.

The way that I was able to access awareness to this fear, and indeed many others... as we all have many of them, was to set the intention to be aware of the limiting beliefs that I held. This intention, of course, had energy, and the ever-supportive Universe assisted me by giving me many opportunities to look at how this fearful part of me created my reality. As I became more aware of when this part of me was active, by feeling what was happening in my physical body, it was then possible for me to step back and see that there might be different choices to be made. I could act or react differently. I could then choose the road I wanted to drive on, and know which freeway to merge onto. I could re-act and not do anything different from the countless other opportunities that I had had in my life, and stay on the freeway to self-judgment or I could consider merging onto a road of possibility, which could initiate much deeper learning.

I learned that when these self-debasing parts of me were active, I had certain feelings in my body. I felt certain fear-based emotions as a distinct constriction in my throat. I set an intention to be aware of what I was feeling inside me. I learned that my body was talking to me. I was able to connect some dots in terms of when I felt the same way before. When I was aware of the fear in me, I began to understand that I was at a crossroads for choice. I found myself feeling very excited about that! I could effect change in my life and see how I was being supported by the Universe to experience my potential!

In these moments of self-discovery and growth, I also became very aware of other senses that I had forgotten. I remembered that I have strong intuition. I was always dreaming things happening before they became reality. I seemed to be tuned in when someone was about to have a crisis in his or her life. An old friend or acquaintance would pop into my thoughts, and within a few days, I would run into them or get a phone call from them. I felt certain things when walking into a room of strangers. I could feel the pain of others. I set an intention to learn about myself as I explored this phenomenon in me. I soon learned that others had these experiences too, and it was really exciting sharing these ideas and insights with them.

I also realized that there was a force working in conjunction with me as I created. I call this force the Universe. I feel that we are all able to tap into this no matter what we might call it: God, Source, or the Creator... This co-creative force is always behind us, supporting our intentions, offering us opportunities for growth.

I was also aware that the more I was open to this support, the more peaceful I felt. I understood that my life happened *for* me not *to* me.

This realization opened me up to energy work and shamanic practices. I realized that I was being guided to take a very strong leap of faith into something that was not a job... not a career... but a calling. And it was calling me into my life!

I was lucky when I made this discovery about myself. I live in a rural setting, with lots of opportunities to be in nature and reconnect with Mother Earth. I began a daily practice and after studying with an amazing teacher, Sandra Ingerman, I was assisting others in their healing, holding celebrations and hosting shamanic workshops at our property.

What became apparent to me after assisting others and hosting events was that those who lived in the cities felt that they could not stay connected to the earth once they returned home. Some people have even shied away from attending any sort of workshop or healing session, because they were instantly frustrated by the thought that, by living in an urban setting, they could not possibly continue this work on their own. They were stopped in their tracks like a traffic jam on the highway, not able to see an off ramp.

Some participants at a workshop felt that the event or retreat had exposed them to parts of themselves that were longing to be nurtured. Once back in their "real world", this longing was forgotten. I have experienced this at retreats myself, and I realized something very important... it is necessary as we raise consciousness to create rituals in our lives that make our lives a meditation. We need to remember daily how precious we are, and find ways to see ourselves in our wholeness. We must see ourselves as the beautiful lights that we are! We are required to live our best life no matter where we are living in the world.

I realized, when working with others in my practice, listening to their complaints, that there was a real disconnect for these people. They were disconnected from nature and all the healing aspects of what nature has to offer, beginning with their own bodies.

The human condition seems to be fraught with the need to find all our faults, judge ourselves and constantly feed the fear-based parts of us. During a workshop or retreat or in a healing session, we get glimpses of our true selves. We may find some compassion for ourselves or remember the gifts that we have to share with others in this precious lifetime. As soon as we arrive home, revived and re-energized, full of insights and love for ourselves and others, we begin to relapse into our unconscious patterns of limiting self-talk, putting other people or our jobs ahead of our own growth, distracting ourselves with our busy lives, and allowing our fearful egos to start to run the show again.

We race back to work, our family and friends. These may be the very distractions that feed the parts of us that are not interested in our growth. We compartmentalize our lives and feel that we cannot possibly act the same way we might do with a workshop full of spiritual friends as we would with our co-workers. We are different people depending on where we are and whom we are with.

We create distance from the authentic and divine self that is the loving part of us – the heartfelt aspect that we all have within – by living these busy, disconnected lives. What can we do to hold on to love? All the connections that we may have felt walking on the land during a retreat or the relaxation created in a healing session melts away when we get back into our vehicles or walk back into the concrete world of the urban dweller.

Where can we go when we truly set our intention to deepen our experience here, no matter where we live? The answer lies inside. As we connect to our natural environment and ourselves more deeply, no matter where that environment is, we can explore and find the peaceful place within us. This serves us as we find our authenticity is alive and well in our tranquility.

Chapter Two

Sacred Space – or Wow,
I Found a Great Parking Space!

All of the work shared in this book is a reminder. It is a reminder of what a precious being you are, and how much the Universe loves you. It is a reminder of the powerful creator that you are, and how you are creating your reality. It is a reminder of your absolute right to be joyful, happy and passionate about your life!

Rituals are powerful ways to remind us of our preciousness. As we engage in our life with intention and openness, we begin to explore our life through ritual. We all have ritual in our lives, but are not always conscious of them. Our practice of setting the alarm for work may be a ritual. Perhaps we read when we go to bed at night. Our morning routine of showering, dressing, brushing our teeth and drinking our coffee on the drive to work is all ritual. Driving a certain route to work or arranging items on our desk or placing the furniture in our office in a certain way are all parts of a ritual. It is probably not conscious. If we have been practicing a certain religion, perhaps we have engaged in prayer as a ritual. Or we may "religiously" attend a yoga class or exercise class, as we know it feels good to do so. These are the sorts of rituals that we can explore when we are considering our spiritual growth and a path to a more peaceful and fulfilling life. If we take the time to perform these rituals daily, then how about adding some that will serve our spiritual selves and well-being?

The first step in creating more meaning in our life is to have a special and precious space to do our "work" that reflects our preciousness. This space is your sanctuary: a place that you can be with yourself in a meaningful, reflective moment each day.

It doesn't matter if you live in the city, on a farm, or halfway up the side of a mountain to do this work. You can have a wonderful growth-filled experience no matter where you live. You will connect with your Guidance, and learn fantastic things to affect your personal growth. You really don't have to go to Italy to eat, India to pray, or Bali to Love!

Many call their sacred spaces "altars", and there is a great amount of joy in creating these special places in your home. Don't feel afraid if you only have a small living space. I have seen some very creative altars made that slip in to a small space. Some are so creative and beautiful that they form part of the decor in the room. Not everyone has a spare room that they can use for meditation and relaxation and so it is important to be able to create your sanctuary no matter what your living space is like. Consider a portable altar, carefully wrapped in a beautiful cloth, on a tray that is moved onto the coffee table for ceremonies, or an altar housed in a lovely jewelry box that is moved to the living room for the ritual or meditation. Your altar may not be able to be visible all the time, due to space constraints, roommates or small children. Perhaps, make use of a cupboard or wall unit, which can be opened during your personal transformation work. I have even seen amazing altars created in a bathroom, as the designer found this to be the only place they could have privacy from roommates, spouses or children.

There are items on an altar that I feel are important. In this study, we are reconnecting to nature and the natural world, which assists us in grounding and finding our true selves. Any sacred space should reflect the intention. It should also reflect you, and your goals for your spiritual growth and change. Your altar will grow as you grow.

When I attend or hold workshops, we create an altar in the center of the room. The altar is created with reverence, with healing as an intention. A beautiful cloth or mat is laid down in the center of the circle. The *elements*, which I will discuss at length later in this book, are always a part of the altar. A candle in the center of the altar represents *fire*. The candle is lit from the moment that we begin our workshop day, and blown out when we finish the sessions. A feather represents *air*. I add crystals for healing and to represent the *earth* element. I put a small globe on the altar that represents and honors our Mother Earth. As we generally work in my workshops to assist in the healing of the planet Earth, this globe represents the receipt of this healing. I also place a bowl or bottle of *water* on the altar.

I have a smudge (a bundle of aromatic and sacred dried herbs) that is lit as I invoke the support of the non-physical beings and the helping spirits. The smudge can also be used by any of the attendees. As the workshop progresses, people add their own precious items or tools that they work with to the altar. I invite them to add items that they use in their own healing practices, or on their own altars at home, as the vibration of the articles will be shifted in the workshop. The healing energy that is present is powerful and affects everything in the room! Participants present jewelry, stones, feathers, fetishes, crystals, and other precious personal items to the altar. If there are friends or family that the participants want to support, I encourage them to place the name of that person under the cloth of this sacred centerpiece. They must have the permission of the person whose name they have submitted, as this is a very important aspect of intention and energy for healing, and essential in shamanic ethics. I will talk much more about this in due time.

For your altar, consider what you wish to connect to, and what you consider to be your goals. If you intend peace in your life, what represents peace to you? Perhaps a picture of the Dalai Lama would inspire this feeling in you. Or consider a photo of a favorite tranquil place in nature. Connect with the natural elements: air, water, fire and earth. This is a means of reconnecting to all things, and is a strong and beautiful intention to hold. What brings you joy? Placing a picture of your family, spouse, or a well-loved pet might bring a smile on your face or warmth in your heart. Is there something that you want to create?

This is a wonderful location for a vision board, or a paper with significant words placed prominently on your altar, or even under your altar cloth. Make this a beautiful space for contemplation, reflection and a sense of unlimited possibility.

Have some sort of smudge with which to clear your space every time you are intending to work on your growth. I use sage, sweet grass, cedar, lavender, Palo Santos, or incense, all of which are readily available at most metaphysical stores. Some people react negatively to smoke, so have sprays made from pure essential oils of the same sacred plants and herbs available for use.

People share that they do not feel they can have or create sacred space at work. Although it may be more difficult, depending on your situation, let me offer you some suggestions to make your workspace more sacred and honoring of you.

I worked in several different office towers in a large city over my long corporate career, and was employed by some fairly conservative oil and gas companies. Some workspaces offered an open concept environment, with very little privacy. I personalized my space. I tacked a beautiful picture of nature right in front of me, so that when I looked up from my work, that beautiful image was what I saw. I would pin feathers or flowers that I found in nature to my cubicle walls. I put tiny animal fetishes on top of my computer, or on my adding machine. I also made my screen saver an image or picture that made me feel calm. I did all of these things with the intention to make the space supportive for me in offering the peacefulness that I wished to create in my life.

In one office, I put up a poster of a window, which looked out to a beautiful green meadow with a stunning blue sky. I brought nature in to my space, because I could not see it from my office. I did not do this from a want or need or a sense of victimhood, but because I sensed that if I invited this beauty into my space, it reflected the beauty in me! I also frequently bought myself flowers, and always had a plant that I nurtured on my desk.

I was lucky in the latter part of my corporate career to have outside offices with big windows and a view, which was really lovely, but I still needed to remind myself to look up from my computer and connect with that beauty during my day. It is very easy to forget to do that on busy days, filled with deadlines. My morning ritual upon arriving at work, was to turn on quiet music on my radio or computer and set intentions while I drank my latte. I was always very early for work. Arriving early was intentional on my part, in an effort to reduce the stress that I felt inside me should I run late. I also arrived before most of my staff, so this was a time I could be with myself, without too many distractions, organize some tasks and be clear about what I was intending to accomplish in the day.

I encouraged my staff to bring in items to personalize their space, and make it comfortable and homey for them. One person brought a salt lamp, which offered soft light, and placed it near her computer. These beautiful lamps, with their healing qualities, cleared the space of negative or misplaced energy. Many brought in pictures of their families, pets, or friends, which I felt helped them in sensing a more nurturing and gentle mood in their workspaces.

We also had times when we smudged the work area. What I would call a happy accident happened one day when I was walking through our department one morning, after a particularly difficult meeting. The energy in our group felt heavy and sullen. I was thinking about how to shift that, and said that I would smudge the office at the weekend. I didn't realize that I had said that out loud, until the woman at the desk that I just passed said, "Great, what time?" We organized the ceremony for the upcoming weekend, after my "accidental" remark.

It was such an eye-opener to me, a great reminder that we forget that we always have support, even during our workday. The Universe had assisted me in creating a beautiful circle with my co-workers, where we set an intention to clear any negative energy, and then open our space to joy and productivity in a healthy way. From that moment, we began to create a community of people who worked together from a much different perspective than most "usual" accounting departments. After that experience, which was certainly a new one for some of the participants, we performed the ceremony a few more times before I left that job.

Did every day go like a peaceful walk in the woods? Absolutely not! Remember the Universe was supporting me in learning about myself, so indeed some days seemed to fall off the rails, as I was supported in challenging my own personal fears. I recognized that we cannot remain parked in a comfortable place. That comfortable place becomes uncomfortable after time and, on most days, I did make a choice to start my day with honoring the parts of me that created peace within.

Whatever your situation, you can create a sanctuary for your inner work, if you choose to. This work is driven by your intention and commitment, and once this is set, your intuition and Guidance will assist you in creating the perfect place for you.

Chapter Three

And So We Begin – or –
Packing the Car for the Trip!

You have created your sanctuary, and you are committed to exploring in search of this elusive "peacefulness". So how does one begin?

What we are endeavoring to accomplish is for you to find a ritual practice that honors you, supports you in your spiritual growth and allows you to open to all the potential and possibilities that you may be offered in this lifetime. As we all are powerful creators of our own reality, it behooves us to understand why we are creating what we are experiencing, and what opportunities for learning the Universe is offering us. We are in partnership with this loving entity, and it supports our intentions one hundred percent.

Shamans have been telling us for thousands of years now that we are dreaming the wrong dream. We are creating war and economic failure, and our lives are filled with materialistic goals. We have been creating with fear, rarely with any awareness or consciousness. We have been feeling our state of lack and want and have been creating our reality from those states. How often have you thought, if I only had more money, things would be better? Or, if I had a different/better/more loving partner, I would be happier? Or, if the Earth weren't so polluted, my children would be safer? These thoughts are coming from parts of us that do not understand that our lives are happening for us to learn about ourselves, and we are not taking responsibility for creating a dream that does serve humanity and ourselves in a more positive way. A very popular saying, originally stated by Ghandi is to "be the change that you wish to see". This is a concept we need to understand, and begin to put into our practice with love, truth and reverence.

I am not saying that if you begin a daily practice and ask for material transformation that you won't receive it. It just seems as though this would be rather fearful, since greed and selfishness are both fear-based emotions, creating reality in that way.

How then to use these incredible gifts of creating with love for our spiritual betterment?

It all begins with considering the love that you have or could have for yourself, and to treat yourself with compassion.

It seems like we are losing the power of our imagination. Imagination was very important when I was a child, but it seems that with television, computers and the process of growing up, our imagination is being lost. The imagination employed when reading versus watching the same story being illustrated on TV is vastly reduced. We are not exercising this important part of us.

In the last chapter, I told you about an office that I occupied for a time. It was a small, inner office, and I could not see outside to even check on the weather. Sometimes, it felt like the walls were coming in on me. One day, while shopping, I saw that beautiful poster I shared about previously. It was a picture of a window, and the viewer looked out on a stunning sunny day. When I put this poster up in my office, I placed it right beside me, where I sat working on my computer all day. All I had to do was glance slightly to my left and I could be transported into that beautiful scene. I could imagine the warmth of the sun, and hear the birds in the trees. I could reconnect with the earth, which I knew fed my soul. I could remember that I was part of that beautiful scene, and this created sensations in my body, of which I was very aware. These sensations felt good. I did not look at this picture with a sense of lack. I did not covet the experience of being outside in that beautiful place. I looked at this picture and I was there, feeling the beauty of the moment, and allowing it to be part of my experience in that moment. This nurtured me, so that I was energized and able to return to my tasks at work without feeling sorry for myself, or wanting to be outdoors. I did not feel stuck in my job. When I used my imagination, and integrated all that it could offer, I felt connected to a world of infinite possibility.

The path of shamanism is a path of direct and meaningful revelation – that is to say you will be tapping into and communicating with helping spirits and Guidance that will give you answers to your questions and a direction to follow, should you choose it. You are able to ask questions and you will receive insights. You will begin creating a life where you are not merely surviving: sitting in traffic, frustrated and angry, or floating through your workday without passion or purpose in order to collect your paycheck. Instead you have an opportunity to thrive. You may still be sitting in traffic, but the lessons, insights and growth that are available for you even within that context may astound you. Your drive to work may become one of the most productive times of your day with respect to your spiritual growth. You might shift your perspective and move out of drudgery and the mundane in your workday. You will be dreaming a new dream. You will be reconnecting to the forces of nature that sustain us and keep us healthy.

To begin, consider the beauty and preciousness of your soul. This may seem vague and difficult at first. Take a moment each morning, before engaging in your busy day. I began this process by beginning to consider my own preciousness before my feet hit the ground running each day. I was just coming out of that groggy, blissful sleep state. I had created a small altar on my nightstand. Lying on my back, still just waking up, I took four conscious breaths. I followed my breath as it entered my body, then felt my breath warmed by my body before I exhaled. Then I set an intention for the day.

At the beginning of this simple practice, I would set an intention to breathe. That was it: to have the awareness and gain *more* awareness about how many conscious breaths I took in the day. I found out early in the process that it wasn't many! I came to know that when I set an intention, that intention had energy, and this energy would evoke the Universe to support me.

The Universe did support me, and sometimes I would be "reminded" in the middle of a board meeting, or in an interaction with a co-worker that I was not breathing consciously. Imagine, in an important and high-level meeting with the president of the company, I was able to be in direct contact with my Guidance and my most wise self! I would be given a clue, a reminder that I wasn't breathing with awareness, for indeed sometimes, especially in times of stress, I would be holding my breath or breathing very shallowly. Someone would say something that would nudge me into the present moment. I might have been vacating, drifting off and thinking about tasks that needed to be accomplished outside of the meeting, wondering what crises had occurred in my absence, or perhaps I was preparing my response to the information being presented. Whatever the case, I was not engaged in the moment. The Universe might remind me by having someone drop something on the floor loudly, bringing my attention back. Perhaps my stomach would growl, and I would be drawn back from my daydream. Perhaps someone would say something that would pique my thoughts.

Whatever the case, because I had consciously set an intention to breathe, I would be supported by the Universe. If I was listening, I could respond. I could take four deep conscious breaths, and refocus on what was going on around me and in me.

I became more able to set intentions that challenged me more deeply. I understood and trusted that the Universe was supporting me. It started out with a realization that I could trust, then was in awe when I saw that I was being offered an opportunity for growth. Then I began to understand more deeply what the Universe was trying to show me. As I became more deeply aware that I was acting compassionately toward myself and the

Universe was supporting *that* intention, I could look at my job, my life, and yes, even a traffic jam from a different perspective. These circumstances were teaching me so much about myself, because I was ready to learn and change myself. I understood that I was the only thing in the equation that I had any control over, and by being clear on intention, and having the courage to consider change, I was shifting my reality.

Of course, I was reading everything I could get my hands on about the subject, and studying and practicing to the best of my ability. Naturally, there were days when I fell into my old patterns. I still do. I have gone into self-judgment about these "lapses", recognized the feelings in my body that I sense when I am engaged in this self-abasement, and challenged myself as best I could not to continue to judge myself. I made a conscious effort to shift my thoughts to what I am learning about myself in the moment. It is the only way to grow. My judgments of my own imperfection can only limit me, and I strive to move forward with gratitude and forgiveness to myself first.

As I practiced more and more with intention, another door opened. I had read about shamanism fifteen or twenty years before, and was interested, but never followed up on anything. On one particular day, I had set an intention to deepen my self-awareness, and open myself to Guidance in a way that I hadn't before. It was clear to me that there was so much *more* that I couldn't interpret with my five senses, and I was open to exploring *that*. I had realized that I was quite intuitive, and this sense was taking me to places that my thinking mind did not think were possible.

I had been away at a retreat in Oregon and, on my return, had a stopover in Portland. There is an amazing bookstore there, which I visited to see what would fall off the shelf for me. With my intention to explore more deeply with Guidance, I found myself picking up books about shamanic journeying and other shamanic practices. The following day, I was researching these books and some of the background information on the authors, and found myself drawn to a workshop with Sandra Ingerman. The Universe was supporting me again!

Perhaps you have been sitting in traffic not noticing what is going on around you, or not feeling as if you are the one in the driver's seat of your own life. I encourage you to start with the two-minute meditation I talked about earlier, before you get up in the morning. What would you like to accomplish in a day? What would serve you in your growth? Perhaps your first simple intention could be to breathe consciously, as mine was, or you could set an intention to discover what would assist you in your growth? I know that you will be supported, and this is the first step toward honoring your soul and your highest self. This is the first step in not just making it through each day, but thriving and nurturing this true self.

When you are ready to spend a little more time, consider the following meditation. It might take a mere five to seven minutes to run through, but I encourage you to experiment with this for yourself.

Meditation

Before getting out of bed in the morning, before letting your feet hit the ground running, lay quietly on your back. Follow your breathing: not controlling your breath, but just noticing your own unique pattern of breathing in and breathing out. Place one palm gently on your belly, just below your navel. Place the other palm on your solar plexus area, just above the navel, and below the heart. Feel your breath raise and lower these areas under your hands. Feel the expansion and contraction of these areas as you breathe. Feel how alive you are as you breathe. What intention do you wish to express for this day... perhaps it can the gentle and simple intention I mentioned above. "Today it is my intention to breathe consciously, with awareness". After a minute or so, move the lower hand to the center of your chest, near your heart, and rest the palm there. Feel the breath flowing gently in these areas, under your hands. Feel the rise and fall of your heart area and your solar plexus area. Reaffirm your intention. After a moment, move the hand that is on your solar plexus and lay the palm gently touching the throat area. Feel your breath as it moves through the throat and then to the heart. Feel the release as you let go on the out breath. After a minute or so, move the hand from your heart to the forehead. Reaffirm your intention. Notice how you are breathing. Let your hands gently move to your sides and notice how your body feels. With a momentary gift of presence and consciousness, you are now ready to start your day in a much different way.

This exercise is a very powerful way to begin the day, and it is also a way to end it. Consider repeating the exercise as you get into bed and prepare for the dreamtime.

If lying in bed doesn't focus you to begin working on yourself in a loving way, consider practicing the meditation at your altar. Perhaps a new part of your daily routine could be to light a candle and sit in its soft light while you set an intention for the day and consciously breathe. Don't forget to blow the candle out when you leave for work, for safety reasons. This precious time in the present moment, or learning to *be* in the present moment, is a true gift for you. You are important and your life is important. Begin by making *you* the most important thing at the beginning of the day by honoring yourself in this small way! The more we can allow ourselves time to be in the present, with our love directed to ourselves, we begin to face the truth: we are worthy, and we are powerfully creating our life.

Chapter Four

Reconnecting With the Cycles – or – The Wheels on the Bus Go Round and Round

Aboriginal people the world over recognize the cycles of life. Each year is marked by seasons following seasons. Each day is marked with a rising sun and a setting sun. Each person's life has a beginning and an end. Women sense the cyclic nature of existence with their monthly menstrual cycles.

In an urban environment, it might be easy to forget about this cyclic nature. We have artificial light in our homes and offices. We have artificial heating to keep these spaces at the same temperature daily. In this relatively artificial world, we forget to honor the very planet that supports our life and the sun that warms us and feeds that life. In the large urban center near my home, the high-rise towers are connected by enclosed walkways that allow people to walk to meetings across the downtown area without going outside at all. Never a breath of outside air during the workday, and if they happen to live in an apartment building connected to this walkway system, people may not leave the confines of this environment from one week to the next. How can these isolated souls possibly connect to the Earth or nature? First and foremost, there must be a connection with self and the bright, beautiful energetic beings that they are.

To honor self, and the cyclic nature in which we thrive, a commitment and intention must first be set. Will you allow yourself to embark on this exploration, this journey to find deeper truth about yourself, how you are connected to Spirit, and glimpse the potential that you possess?

If your answer is yes, you can step into truly experiencing your life as a ritual – a meditation if you will – so that in your finite physical life cycle on Earth, you will create with depth and meaning.

As we explored in the previous chapter, we can begin with honoring the daily cycle. Waking up in the morning is a perfect time to set intention, be present and honor *you*, even for a few moments. I trust that by this chapter, you are giving yourself a gift of a few precious moments to be with yourself. This is the beginning of the process. There is no judgment, no pressure, just a few precious moments of celebrating the self. Remember that you can also unwind and set an intention to let go of things that don't serve you when you are readying yourself for bed.

The dreamtime is an important part of the daily cycle. I invite you to set the intention to remember your dreams and begin to tune into them more deeply. They are giving you brilliant messages and Guidance. In our busy lives, where we may be chronically sleep deprived, becoming deeply rooted in this balancing time of our cycle is paramount to well-being. Once you begin traveling this road of self-awareness, you may find the messages in your dreams are quite profound and enlightening. Some people keep a dream journal. This is a helpful way to track similarities of themes within your dreams. Within these themes are the possibilities of great understanding. I find it helpful to have a pen and paper beside my bed to use when I wake up from a dream. I can jot some key words down on the pad of paper, barely waking myself up. Many times I have gotten out of bed after having a particularly colorful or amazing dream to have forgotten it by the time I left for work.

After a month or so goes by, with daily practice (or the closest to daily you can manage), let us begin to look at the monthly cycles that we experience. As mentioned, women are quite well reminded on this cyclical nature of their month, but may not be really tuned into it. Because of hormone cycles controlled artificially with the use of birth control pills or hormone patches, women's inner clocks may not be tuned in to the natural cycles, when we were influenced by the cycles of the moon. We can reconnect to this natural cycle by following and honoring the moon cycles. It is really important that we reconnect to the natural forces in our lives.

We can be so disconnected to nature and the flow of life that we don't even notice that it is the full moon, but you have only to check with any of your friends that work in a hospital or a police station to know the effect it can have on people. Once you find out when the next full moon is occurring, check to see how *you* feel as you move toward that time. Many find that they are restless or begin to have a bit of insomnia. Some say they have more energy and are more productive or creative. Begin to follow your own unique response to this awesome and brilliant natural reminder.

In an urban environment, it might be difficult to see the moon coming to its fullness in the night sky. Your apartment may not face the right direction or there might be too much streetlighting to see the heavenly bodies. This is not an issue, once you have established your intention. Allow quietness within yourself and set the intention to connect to the phases of the moon. What do you appreciate about the moon? What do you love about the changing faces of this beautiful sphere of light? Perhaps you remember that the light of the moon is a reflection of the sun's light? What is reflected through you? Do you feel the changes of energy in your co-workers as the moon shifts in its cycle? Whatever you love about the moon, consider this ritual at the next full moon.

Full moon ritual

Stand in your favorite place in your home: your sanctuary, or your altar. If you have a view of the moon, or even a reflection of it, consider opening your curtains to see it in its radiance. Perhaps light a candle to represent the light of the moon if the direct light is not available to you. (Candles are always appropriate in a ceremony or ritual, no matter what, but for this ceremony, they may have a very specific relevance!) Play soft music or sing a lullaby to the moon. Allow yourself to feel sensations in your body. Do you feel your heartbeat? Do you notice your breathing? Are you gently swaying or moving as you sing or listen to the music? Let your mind become quiet. As you reconnect with the breath, is there a difference in the way that your body feels as you softly stand in the presence of the moon? Gently speak to the energy of this beautiful entity. Tell the moon what you appreciate about her. I love to share with the moon that I appreciate how she lights up the landscape at night. From my window, I see the light shimmer on the trees and fields. I love the moon's effect on the animals, especially the coyotes and wolves, who sing to her. Their songs are my lullabies as I settle into bed. Grandmother moon's light is a reflection of the light from the sun. There are powerful insights in considering what we reflect to others and what they might reflect to us.

There are many CDs with the sounds of nature on them. These may help you find your story of gratitude for the moon. Remember that there are people all around the world that honor the cycles of the moon. Open yourself to the possibly that you can connect with them now, and feel what happens in your heart. Allow yourself to be an observer, not judging or thinking about this. Just feel and consider the possibility. This can be fun and exciting, and is not mentioned here just so that you find one more thing to worry about. *Experiment with the possibility.* Perhaps you have a friend or colleague or a relative somewhere in the world that you could attempt to share this exercise with, and you can talk together about what happened for both of you after your ritual.

Participate in the ceremony for perhaps ten or fifteen minutes, unless you are really feeling a deep connection with the full moon, in which case, go with your feelings! Stay as long as you need. You will never go anywhere that you will not return safely.

If you get "lost" in your meditation, remember your intention. Repeat it in your mind. Be gentle with yourself. Allow yourself to take baby steps back to the natural world and all its gifts.

When you are engaged in the busy-ness of your life, it is sometimes difficult to remember to practice deepening your relationship with yourself. Be reminded of the purpose for doing anything that honors and celebrates you and the world that you live in, and the co-creative partner that you have by your side – the Universe. These practices nurture your soul, and support you in your journey.

As you begin to acknowledge all the cycles that you can participate in and, indeed, are a part of you, you will find yourself noticing more of them to cherish. The moon has several important phases in her cycle that you can experience. After practicing with the full moon cycles, find out when the new moon occurs. Set out a sacred time for you to honor this part of the cycle of Grandmother Moon.

The *new moon* is a time of rebirth and renewal of energy. As mentioned earlier, the moon is very influential on our state of being and our energy. The new moon begins a new cycle of growth and potential. This is a powerful time to set an intention, start a new project, begin a new life habit, or consider a new and more loving belief for you or for your life path. This is the beginning of a wonderful cycle to manifest something in your life.

Again, you may not be able to see the tiny sliver of light in the sky that is the moon returning to the night sky, especially if you live in the bright lights of the city, but by consulting your computer or calendar, you can certainly determine when the new moon is occurring. The dates of each full moon and new moon are the same all over the world, although each country's clock could show a different time because of time zones.

Always begin at your place of ritual in your home, and set the stage for your ceremony. Light a candle, and have some sage ready to light. Remember to be safe with fires and smoke. I burn my sage in a deep shell or a rock with a deep indentation, so there is no danger of it igniting a fire on the carpet or on clothing.

New moon ritual

Imagine the returning light of the moon in the night sky, or if you do see her, face her, and welcome its return by smiling at her. Allow yourself to follow your breathing, settling into your own rhythm. Notice how your body feels as you become present with this powerful being of emerging light in the sky. Welcome the moon as she returns to us. Many aboriginal people call the moon Grandmother. As you reflect on your day, your week, or the past month, how do you want the moon to support you going forward? Are you beginning to make some changes in your life through reconnecting to your inner being, the moon, or to nature? She could help you with staying on track, or deepening your practice. Light your sage or smudge and send the smoke to her with your intentions. Keep noticing what you are feeling in your body.

See these few precious moments of existing from the perspective of the emerging light and the energy of the moon. Allowing yourself to be a part of this natural cycle can shift your energy profoundly. Just being present for those moments, while considering your preciousness, is a poignant experience filled with limitless possibility.

Thank the moon for her support and sit for a moment in silence, considering the light from the candle and imagining your dreams, prayers or intentions reaching the moon on the smoke from your smudge. Feel the gratitude in your being. You have made a new start.

The rituals given so far have the potential to initiate big changes in your life. Use your imagination to create moon cycle rituals, for example, if you began a new project at the new moon; celebrate the completion, or your ongoing commitment to the project, at the full moon.

These special times of awareness in the present moment, reconnecting with our powerful cyclic nature, are a start to reconnecting with your soul, and the powerful creator that you are when you work in alliance with the Universe. Remember that you are creating your reality. You have unlimited potential, and now you are beginning to sense that there is more to you than being the employee, the partner, the parent, the daughter or son, or so on. This outer shell that you present to the world is not all of who you are.

Let's deepen your work now, and have you meet some non-physical helpers that will support, teach, guide and accompany you.

Chapter Five

Meeting your Spirit Helpers – or – Now I Use the High Occupancy Lane

Perhaps as you have been getting to know yourself better each day with your new daily rituals, you are sensing that there is more there than just your own energy. Perhaps you have felt or seen or just know that there is more. Here is the good news! The shamanic life is a path of direct revelation – you get information and guidance directly from the Source, your guides and your non-physical teachers. This information is specifically for you, and you can ask anything. This deeper connection to your own personal helping spirits is a healing path of wisdom, connection and wonder. Your helping spirits have your highest and best interests at heart.

It is not just shamans who had helping spirits and Guidance to help their tribes find food, shelter and health over the millennia. Historically, this particular member of the group was perhaps the one who had the most developed skills in these areas, and through a generational lineage or specific teachings, he or she would perform these critical roles in the community.

In our times today, these specific services are not necessarily required from our guides. We have nonetheless tended to forget that we do have these powerful allies of our own for our other needs. We all have Guidance in some form or another. All of us have connection to our helping spirits, but over the years, we have forgotten this. We have been busy thinking that we are alone here, thinking for ourselves, and generally thinking, thinking, thinking. Our brains can be a very interesting place – full of polarity (the brain has two sides, so of course there is duality and polarity). We have been developing our left brain, which is wonderful for logical, pragmatic thinking, but we have not generally been stimulating our right brain – our creative side. This is the more female side of our brain, and it assists us in a different type of thinking. The capacity of our brain is limited, and even though we use a very small portion of it, we would be served so much more meaningfully if we opened ourselves up to the limitless Universal wisdom.

In the right brain, we have more of a *feeling* aspect and we can sense or "know" from our intuition. It may not be logical, but it is very powerful. This is the side of the brain that is most creative. It has more feminine qualities in that it uses feelings, symbols and images in processing. It is the side where imagination is the ruler. It is the side of the brain that considers the bigger sense of things, the global picture, the expansiveness of creative possibility. It is the side of the brain that tends to be in the present, not thinking about the left brain's important contexts of the past or future. The left brain tends to be the worrier, the planner, and has more apparent "male" tendencies. The right brain senses our connections as a collective, and the left brain considers our differences. So how can we stop the chatter between these polar opposites and get a sense of what is *really* going on? We can connect with our inner Guidance, our divine wisdom and our helping spirits!

So how do you access the road to this direct revelation of which I spoke earlier? Shamans throughout history have used many tools to reach a state of consciousness where they are open to their Guidance in a profound way. Rhythmic drumming, rattling, singing and dancing were all tools to access a trance-like state, which provided the gateway to Non-Ordinary Reality where information and Guidance was afforded. The shaman or medicine man/woman became the "hollow bones", through their chosen means of transforming into that state of openness. By having hollow bones, the shaman reached a state where the ego was dropped. Personality stepped out of the equation, and true wisdom flowed through. Our personality puts filters on information that we might receive from our guides, and it is important that we learn to get our thinking minds out of the way of that flow.

How, in this world that seems to require us to *think* and *do* so much, do we get into contact with this wisdom? Can we achieve this trance state, and enter this arena where the answers are? Who are these helpers that we are supposed to meet?

By now, if you have been practicing the important beginner steps in your inner work, you have established a set of rituals to reconnect with your soul, your true self, the natural world, and its cycles. You may have reached a state of presence or stillness in the moment, and recognized that there is a feeling of expansion there – like you might have found a doorway or passage to somewhere deeper, and more meaningful. It is not that you have left this reality, but you have sensed that there is more available to you than the reality that we walk in every day.

Consider your dreamtime, for instance. You have probably woken up from a wild or crazy dream and felt the "realness" of it. Did it really happen? Have you phoned someone who was in your dream to see if they were OK? The part of you that is more than your five senses has been activated and you have experienced something very real to you. Your Earth-bound personality or ego wasn't in the way, telling you it wasn't possible. Whatever the story was in the dream, it felt real, and you have experienced something as real as being at your desk at work, or sitting in your car in rush hour. You experienced sensations and emotions. If you remembered the dream throughout your day, you may notice that you experienced these same emotions and sensations when you recall the story in your dream. These sensations and emotions are the physical manifestations of the potential meaning or insights that were also part of the dream.

The dreamtime is a reality in its own right. From a shamanic perspective, dreams have metaphoric messages for us. Usually, the story is not to be taken literally, although some experience psychic glimpses into the future. For most of us, it is more about the meaning, the feelings created by the dream, and the lessons that can be learned about ourselves through those stories.

In your brief meditations, you might experience what you might have termed a daydream: a little moment when reality seemed altered. What you experienced in this daydream felt very real. This is another aspect of the dreamscape or dream world, even though we were "awake" for it.

In shamanism, there is another reality that we can step into. If we term our daily life "Ordinary Reality", shamans around the world call the other "Non-Ordinary Reality". Studies by anthropologists and students of shamanism confirm consistencies surrounding Non-Ordinary Reality existing the world over, and anthropological, metaphysical, and theological studies from around the world have documented the similarities of shamanic beliefs no matter what culture or country the shamans came from. Shamans from the four corners of the world believe, visit and have mapped, a Lower World, a Middle World and an Upper World. These worlds have their own magical qualities, hold their own mysteries, and have, living in them, guides, teachers and helpers that are eager to be of assistance to us. So how do we reach these spirit helpers? Intention is always our greatest ally. We must truly desire to connect, converse and listen to our Guidance. We must first also believe in the possibility of their existence!

In Native American cultures, and many other indigenous cultures, it is believed that we all have a power or totem animal that supports and guides us. The traits and qualities of this animal can assist us greatly. When you were young, did you have a teddy bear? Did you have a stuffed animal that you trusted and told all your secrets and stories to? Did you have an affinity or love for certain animals? This may have been an early connection to your power animal or spirit animal. As we grew up we let go of this connection in our thoughts, and through our faltering and ever-diminishing imagination, but perhaps, through the following exploration, you will find that you did not let go of this connection in your heart.

We generally find our power animal spirit in the Lower World. This world is not physically below ours, nor is it "hell" like the name might intimate! It is a place in Non-Ordinary Reality, which typically looks very natural, with trees, mountains, valleys, streams, oceans and the like. Travelers to this realm generally see a sky and land, similar to our own reality.

Now is the time to put the key into the ignition and begin to "journey". Shamanic journeying is the term for traveling through a type of altered meditative state, to Non-Ordinary Reality. It is the vehicle to the virtual drive-in movie of revelations and divination that can be yours to assist you in healing, growing, connecting, learning, teaching, living and thriving in your life with meaning and purpose!

As I mentioned, *intention* is the key to unlocking the door, and setting the GPS. The drum, rattle or rhythmic dance is the engine. The rhythm of the driver – the drum or rattle, for example, is the vehicle that transports you into a theta state of brainwave activity. This state is where we are able to let go of the tethers of our left brain and experience something quite different. It is the state reached in meditation, and has also been studied and revealed to be the mind state achieved by yogis and those others in various types of deep prayer.

When learning to journey, I suggest that you purchase a CD of drumming or rattling and practice with this. After a few times of journeying using drumming CDs, I was moved to drum for myself, and never looked back, but I do feel that there are a number of beginners on this path who find they have more success in their practice while using a CD and headphones. I do encourage you to use headphones, not only because the drumming could disturb your neighbors, but also because you might not be as distracted by outside noises of traffic or your environment as you learn. The outside world can be a noisy place, full of distractions. Be gentle with yourself and considerate of others.

Journeying can be a magical experience! Prepare yourself, just as if you are going on a trip in the car. Pack your car with the necessary items for your journey. To help with visual distraction, cover your eyes with a blindfold. A bandana, tie, or sleep mask makes great eye covering. By using an eye covering, visual distractions are minimized and from a scientific perspective, the darkness created when you cover your eyes stimulates the pineal gland in the same way that darkness stimulates us to enter the dream state. Make sure you are comfortable. Sit in a comfortable chair or lie on the floor with a pillow and blanket. This is meant to be a good experience, and should not create physical discomfort. Get your CD ready, and put on your headphones. Have a notebook and pen nearby, as you might want to jot down some of the things that you "see" on your journey.

The intention for this first journey is to meet your spirit animal in the lower world. Experiment with holding your intention. While learning, I sat in silence and repeated my intention so as to instill it in my mind and heart. When learning to journey, it is like learning to meditate without a guide leading you through it – thoughts and worries that take you out of the present moment can distract you. Be patient, and do your best. My advice is to give yourself a time limit of about ten to twelve minutes at first, to get practiced in reaching the lower world. Be sure that your drumming CD has a "call back beat", which will assist you in coming back to the present moment of ordinary reality. The "call back" is a distinct change of the tempo of drumming, given as a cue to draw you back to the starting point of your journey.

Our brains are amazing things, and your amazing brain really doesn't know the difference between this normal reality and our thoughts, our dreams and our visions. They all seem real to the brain. The journey to the Lower World can stimulate physical responses, which may also be a distraction. Be open to whatever happens, and keep feeling that body of yours! It will give you many messages.

We reach the Lower World by entering through a place in nature. This place can be somewhere you have been and loved, or it might be a place that you create within you for this purpose. Generally, we enter into Non-Ordinary Reality through a portal that we recognize in the physical world. For the Lower World, we enter through a cave, a hole in a tree, a rabbit burrow, a body of water, or wherever your imagination may take you. As I mentioned, this portal could be a place that you have visited and remember distinctly, or one that you create.

Many fairy tales or stories from long ago depict shamanic journeys. Hiding their shamanic beliefs in a story was a way for the ancestors to retain their legacy of beliefs in times of political struggles, and also, history was usually retold orally. Read some fairy tales and you will understand what I mean, especially after journeying for a time. Many of these tales are profoundly shamanic. I wonder about dear Alice in Alice in Wonderland as an example of a modern fairy tale. When she went down the rabbit hole, she may have been journeying to the Lower World!

To enter the Lower World, think about something that makes sense to you for traveling downward, just like Alice. In modern times, this could even be an elevator, or driving your car to the bottom level of the underground parking lot. If you enter your journey through water, maybe you will slide down a watery mudslide to the Lower World. Whatever the vehicle, you will probably have a sense of moving downward.

I would note, however, that I am finding in my healing practice and in workshops, that many people are beginning to "find" themselves "there" in the Lower World, just like they popped there automatically. I believe that their intention is very strong, and also that we are so supported by spirit and the vibration of other travelers to this realm, that the more traditional methods are not as relevant for us anymore. Children travel almost instantly to Non-Ordinary Reality, and I believe it is because they have not yet forgotten how easy it is.

I would suggest that the first few times you journey, have your starting point clear and your intention strong in your mind. Envision your entry point as the drumming starts, and with intention, you are on your way. By understanding and practicing this traditional method, if you meet with difficulty, there is a consistent methodology to fall back on.

Allow yourself to *feel* throughout the journey. Most have a feeling of falling, or moving downward. Your intention to meet your spirit animal in the Lower World will keep you from getting lost. Remember to repeat your intention if you notice your thoughts distracting you. Allow your senses to be fully alive. Feel the warmth of the earth as you sink downward. If you are traveling through the roots of a tree, can you smell the earth? Do you sense the twists and turns in the roots as you scurry downward? If you dove into water, is it warm or cold? Does your elevator have lights or is it very dark as you go to the bottom floor? What do you hear as you progress downward?

The typical Lower World journey will feel like falling and then finally moving laterally toward a light-filled opening. At the opening, you might see a vista of a meadow, a mountain valley, a beach, or a beautiful desert. There are no rules for what you will come across, so enjoy the view.

Begin to notice what animals are around you. Your spirit animal may come right up to you to meet you. If you see hawks flying overhead, ask them if they are your power animals. They will answer, or you will know something from their actions or attitude. Don't rush; there is plenty to see here! Don't worry if the hawks say that they are not your power animals. Ask them if they can direct you to the animal that is. If they don't do this, don't take it personally; they are just helping you feel part of this magical place. Be sure to thank them for their assistance.

You may not be a visual person in this realm. I often find that whatever your strongest sense is in normal reality, it is the weakest sense in the non-ordinary realm. Open to all of your senses. Perhaps you can smell the grass, or the trees, or feel the warmth of the sun. Perhaps your hearing is very strong here and you will hear the voice of your power animal. Be open to all the possibilities. This is *very* important. Do not feel like a failure if you don't *see* your power animal on the first try. Many take a number of journeys before they get to know how to work with their more powerful senses in this altered state.

When you do have the good fortune to meet your power animal – and you will, with patience and persistence – be with them. Fly with them, if it is a bird. See the world from their perspective. Swim if you meet a fish or an alligator. See in the dark, if you meet an owl or bat. Their perspective is part of the wisdom that they will impart to you to assist you in this world. This is where the rubber meets the road. You are connecting to a non-physical being that is going to be your ally! Feel what happens in your body when you meet your helper. Do you feel happy? Are you a bit afraid? Is it exciting? Does it feel like you have known this creature all your life, and you are reconnecting with an old friend? Is it scary to fly high about the ground? Does it make your stomach flip over and over to run so fast with a cheetah? These are all things that you can write down in your notebook when you return. If you have time, have a conversation with your new friend and helper. Ask him anything! If it's time, he will give you the answers. You no longer need to feel alone.

The first few journeys will seem very short, and before you know it, the return beat of the drum will be sounding. This is your cue to say thank you to your power animal and take the journey home to Ordinary Reality. You return the way that you went: Up the elevator, slide or pathway back to the opening that you entered. Retrace your steps to your room, and take some time now to write down what happened in your journey.

I cannot stress enough that you should not judge yourself if you feel that you did not meet your animal, especially if it is your first journey. You must be gentle with yourself. I encourage you to write down what did or didn't happen. Did you have unrealistic expectations? Perhaps you will remember a small detail that will confirm your journey out of this reality, even if it seems very small. Did you notice a change in the light inside your eyes as you visited the Lower World? Did the temperature change? Did you feel excited? Relaxed?

One good friend of mine mentioned very recently, after practicing journeying for quite a while with some success, that she had been hearing a flute during her journeying, but never realized that this sound was actually an aspect of her Guidance. She is now developing a stronger sense of her clairaudient abilities. This is one of her strongest senses in Non-Ordinary Reality!

I have had beginners say that all they saw was a big brown eye or a black nose, but they don't know what their animal is. Well, although they may not recognize what these features might be attached to, it isn't a bad place to start from the next time they venture forth in exploration. Perhaps the next time, they will smell the hay that the horse was eating. Maybe they will hear the purr of the big cat. They will hear the growl of the bear, or the howl of the wolf. On the next journey, they might see the eye and then the talon of the eagle or owl. A touch of soft fur will offer a kiss to their outstretched hand. More clues will be given, and the journeys will seem more complete and meaningful over time. Be sure to jot whatever the experience was in your notebook.

Once you have made contact and have met with your power animal a few times, you will realize that journeying can be a very powerful tool. This is indeed the direct revelation that I spoke of earlier. You can ask your helper any question. Be wary, though. Timelines in Non-Ordinary Reality are quite different from ours.

Remember that the messages we get in this other realm are generally metaphoric in nature. So when your power animal shows you are falling off a wall, this is more than likely not an indicator that you are heading for a literal accident, but merely that you might be slightly off your path, or perhaps your life is not in balance. Consider the question that you asked as your intention for the journey, and don't take things literally.

The best questions to ask your helping spirits begin with *who*, *what, where* and *how*. You will notice that there is no *when* and no *why*. These questions may wait until you have more of a rapport with your spirit guide, and understand the intricacies of these types of questions. Practice with the other four until you are clearer.

Also, understand that there are no power animals that are more or less powerful than others. Just because your power animal is a mouse, it doesn't mean that your mouse is not as wise or powerful an ally as your friend's mountain lion. We all seem to have to compare! Everyone wants to have a white wolf or an eagle, or a ferocious grizzly bear, but what if the message that your mouse or tiny bee gives you changes your life? That is possible. All animals are equal in the Universe, just as, on a soul level, we humans are all equal. The message given with love and clarity from the gentle, tiny mouse is just as important and viable as the stately wolf.

Our power animals are not made stronger by their size or fury. They all have attributes that are applicable in our lives. Consider the wolf, who is a family oriented and a loving parent. Observe the mother grizzly bear who protects her young. Feel the love of the African lioness purring as she licks her mate. Envision the perspective of life that an eagle has as he flies high in the sky. He is probably not thinking about minute details, but considers the global perspective. Perhaps his message for you is to step back a bit and be the observer in your life, without obsessing about the small stuff. The silent flight of the owl allows him to go unnoticed as he hunts, and he sees clearly in the dark. His message may be to look beneath the surface to see the truth. The flighty deer may seem like a weak or vulnerable animal, an animal that is preyed upon by those that are stronger, but remember her quickness to respond to a situation, knowing how and when she is safe and can relax and trust. The tiny chipmunk is a busy and industrious fellow, who always has a stash of food for winter. Sense that each animal, big or small, prey or hunter, has its own distinct strength and its messages are going to be tailored specifically for you.

You may be greeted and supported by a mythical animal, like a unicorn or dragon. I wonder what magical messages these helping spirits will share with you? The messages that can be conveyed by a creature that does not exist in our reality might be very transformative. They may inspire you to consider past lives, or the expansiveness of time. Perhaps they will convince you of your own uniqueness, and that magic that is possible by developing your imagination.

Remember that this power animal is yours. It has qualities and attributes that support you and your growth. If you are in a quandary about what this particular totem is bringing for you, try not to think about it too hard. Consider how this animal lives and thrives in its world. Does it have a certain nature? When you look at a picture or image of your power animal, what are your first thoughts or impressions? How do you feel? There are many wonderful books that indicate the ancient or traditional meanings or qualities that specific animals tend to offer. Sometimes these are very valid, and I have used these reference materials in my practice as a basis of sharing insights with my clients, but there is consistently a more personal message or potential strength that is being offered as well. It is highly individual and unique to you.

We may have a central or lifelong power animal, but that helping spirit can change as we change. Others may show up from time to time as we journey through life. Your needs, questions, or requirements may shift and another helper may show up to help you through a certain situation or to navigate a particular storm. Be open to their support. They all show up for a reason. For example, when performing different healing ceremonies, I have different helpers. We all have the team that we require when we need them.

We may have many other spirit guides, some of which may not be in animal form. The journey to find your other helpers usually begins with an exploration of the Upper World.

The Upper World is not "Heaven" as we might think, although some aspects of this realm certainly seem very Heaven-like, complete with white light and the presence of angels. Scholars have also mapped the Upper World, as they interviewed shamans around the globe and discussed this subject with them. There are similar chambers and rooms described by all shamans, no matter where they live. There are dark rooms, light rooms, rooms that resemble ancient lands. There are fields and courtyards and cathedrals, and many other wonderful sites to see.

Throughout the interviews and anthropological research, shamans described a membrane or veil that must be crossed to get to the Upper World. A perfect example of an Upper World journey is the story of Jack and the Beanstalk, where Jack climbed a giant beanstalk, and went through a level of clouds before he reached the land where the Giant's castle appeared to him.

After going through the clouds, Jack was able to step onto a surface just like walking on the ground thousands of feet below. He had broken through the veil (the cloud) to the Upper World. Just as in the Lower World, the Upper World is only spiritual, thus only spiritual beings are there. There are ancestors, ascended masters, teachers, angels, and other compassionate beings waiting to assist us. This is a place that you can visit to meet with your helping spirit, have conversations with them and ask them questions. They know many things about healing and have infinite wisdom to assist you. Let's explore the Upper World.

First of all, you will prepare yourself, just as you did in the Lower World Journey. Be comfortable in your quiet space, without the potential distraction of the phone or a visitor. Light the candle on your altar, and have your area cleared if you choose, by smudging your space. Be ready with your CD of drumming. Have a journeying tract of approximately twelve minutes, with a call back beat at the end. Have your blindfold ready, and your notebook and pen close by. Don't forget your blanket and pillow as you settle into your comfortable position for journeying.

It might seem obvious, but the Upper World is a realm that requires you to travel upward, and as you journey, you might feel the sensations of this upward motion. Open yourself to this possibility, and notice what is going on in your physical body. Do you feel excitement or fear? Just notice... this is all about the experience. Allow yourself to *be* there!

As with the journey to the Lower World, you will likely need a vehicle to get you there, at least at the beginning of your practicing. As I mentioned earlier, I am finding that some people now, through whatever means or vehicle, are finding their way to Non-Ordinary Reality in a less traditional fashion – they are just appearing there. I do feel this is because of the shifts in consciousness that we are making as a whole, but again, let's be sure you have the complete and traditional instructions, so that you will be assured of success in your flight.

Find your entry point and vehicle. An upward journey can be initiated through the same hole in a tree that you may have used for your journey downward to the Lower World, but instead of going down through the roots of the tree, you climb up through the trunk to the branches and leaves. You may ride a tornado, just like Dorothy in *The Wizard of Oz* (another fabulous shamanic story, I must say!) You might run up a rainbow, or jump off a mountainside onto a cloud. You could ride up in a hot air balloon, or soar on the back of a bird. Perhaps you will climb Jack's beanstalk, or a golden ladder, run up a sunbeam or moonbeam, or maybe you will step into your elevator and press *up*. Some journeyers have ridden the back of their spirit animal. Whatever the case, envision your starting place and feel that upward surge of energy. Remember the intention of this initial journey: you are journeying to the Upper World to find a helping spirit. This spirit is your teacher. Please be sure to have this intention clear and concisely in your thoughts in case you are distracted or resistant in any way.

As you journey upward, you will pass through a thin veil or membrane. Remember the clouds in Jack's climb to the Giant's castle? You might feel the stickiness or resistance of the veil, but you will pass through these clouds or the gentle mist. Some experience a layer of amber or a membrane of some type, or step through a curtain. You might feel a change of temperature or a shift in the light. Then you will know that you are in the Upper World.

In most journeys that I have taken, and in those people have shared with me, there is intense light in some of the rooms of the Upper World, and there are many rooms. Some are lighter or darker, some look ancient, and some look modern. Explore, knowing that you are safe in this world, in whatever room or rooms you visit.

Remember your intention. Begin to look for the spirit guide that is your teacher. You may meet several people, and be sure to ask them if they are your helping spirit or guide. You can, of course, speak and interact with these spirits, just as you interact with all of us in normal reality! Don't be put off if they say no, or walk past you. Your guide is there. You might ask some of the others there to direct you to him. Your helping spirit will confirm that he or she is for you, and remember, you can always ask for confirmation.

Just as each power animal is just as equal and powerful as the next, please be sure not to judge your helping spirits. Whether you are having conversations with Jesus or Zeus, or a hobo named Box Car Willie, their wisdom is powerful and specific to you. I have been to gatherings where people have been engaged in an interesting process that I call spiritual name-dropping. One person will share that they are working with an archangel and the next will say, "I have been working with Jesus, and he is so much more powerful than an angel!"

It is so interesting that people feel that their guide must be bigger and better than the next person's, when really, the form that is given to them by their guide is so that the person can be more open to and accepting of the messages that they will receive. Remember that all things that you see in a journey are generally metaphoric in nature. If your hobo helping spirit suddenly gets a new suit or hops on a train, what is he *really* expressing to you? This is a message for you and no one else. It is not about relaying a message to someone else, in an effort to make him or her change behavior, for instance. This message is specifically for you.

There are no hard and fast rules that say power animals only live in the Lower World, or that Guidance with more human-like form takes place only in the Upper World. Be open to experimenting, and open to all the possibilities. The only rule is that there are *no* rules! Sometimes our "power animals" are trees or plants! In Native American lore, the trees are called the Standing People, and have amazing qualities for healing and connection. We merely set these very specific intentions in these early journeys so that you set yourself up for success, and your Guidance really supports that.

It may take two or three journeys to connect with your Guidance, especially if you are doing relatively short journeys of ten to twelve minutes as suggested. Sometimes, your commitment is being challenged. You might even be being challenged by your ego to see how committed you are to opening to a more healthy and loving way of being! Don't be discouraged. Keep your notes and your open heart. This is something that you probably haven't ever done in your life. You might not have done this for a very long time, if, by chance, you did journey with your imagination as a child. Always be gentle with yourself.

Once connected, you can visit any time. Don't be surprised if, after a time, your power animal or your guide wishes to travel back with you. You can always carry their loving spirit in your heart.

Chapter Six

Are there Bad Days to Journey?
– or – The Bumps on the Road

You can establish quite a connection with your helping spirits. Don't worry about offending them or posing to them a question that they can't handle. If it appears that they are not giving you the answer you want, check your intention. Did you have an expectation that was not realistic, or have an attachment to receiving a certain answer?

As in all journeys, this is sacred work, and your honor, gratitude, and reverence while connecting with these allies is essential, just as is your intention. Ask for assistance to establish if your intention is of an ill or fear-based nature. Remind yourself that all of us, and indeed every single thing in every reality, is an energetic being, as are your spirit helpers; understand that you will attract what your thoughts and energy are emitting. Please be sure that you are feeling clear about your intention, and that if you are seeking validation from outside yourself, there is no spirit helper that can make you feel complete.

I suggest that you have a good understanding of intention and are on a path of self-discovery from an aspect of self-love and compassion when you are engaged in these journeys. Please be sure that you are not asking your guides how you will become rich, or how to become "perfect". Interestingly enough, these are not necessarily things that they will understand from the same viewpoint as we might in this realm. From the perspective of the Universe or your Guidance, your experience on this Earth School is always perfect and rich. Your life is perfect to learn about what you incarnated to heal and understand in this lifetime. You are rich with opportunities to learn about yourself and abundant with support from your guides.

Your experience here is in line with the lessons and under-standings that you signed up for when you incarnated into this lifetime. If you were meant to understand about trust, you will be given many experiences to challenge your trust while in the Earth School. So, if you are asking your helping spirits for the perfect life partner, imagine what you may be co-creating with the Universe. The perfect partner for your particular soul's learning may teach tons about trust by being the most unethical, lying, and thoughtless creep on the planet. And your spirit guides will have done their best work to assist you! The Universe may provide this "perfect" partner to allow you to learn to trust in the Universe and your own Higher Self. Be specific. It is always the most productive and wise choice to be doing your own inner work, and have your own insights on what questions to ask your guides. When you are ready, and you are clear that you are not seeking approval outside of yourself, for instance, you could ask your helping spirits to assist you in how to attract a bright, compassionate, loving, life partner. Meditate on the qualities that you are looking for and be specific: you are probably not asking for a cat for a companion or loving, faithful dog.

The important point to remember is that you must not give up your part in the precious ability to create. You are asking for *assistance* in co-creating. Allow yourself to ask for assistance from a *loving* place within you. We are all quick to notice what we feel we lack. We are all aware of what we don't want. We tend to forget that we are here to work on an inner growth experience: the remembering of our wholeness. We are expertly trained to notice all of our flaws, but forget our perfection. We forget that we are divine light. In your daily work, consider meditating or journeying to allow your spirit guides to release from you whatever keeps you separate from being your most radiant light.

One of the most powerful journeys that I experienced was a journey I took with my power animal. I had set the intention to receive guidance on how best to release self-judgment. I journeyed to my power animal, visited with her and rode her across a beautiful field. I kept asking my question: how do I release self-judgment? She led me to a beautiful reflecting pool, and walked with me to the side of the pool. She stood beside me and asked me to look at our reflections. She encouraged me to look at our beauty as we stood there.

She asked me to describe what I saw in her. I mentioned her strength, her wisdom, her gentleness, and her compassion. She asked me to consider that she was there to remind me that all of those qualities I saw in her were in me, too. She encouraged me to remember what my reflection in the water looked like as we gazed into the pool. She had me describe my body, which in Non-Ordinary Reality is not quite the body I see in the mirror in this reality. She reminded me that the body I have in her realm is my body without the weight of ego, fear, or doubt attached to it.

She sang an ancient Sufi blessing to me: "You are my beloved. I open my heart to you." I was moved by her words and have held on to the insights that I received from that journey. She reminds me often to look at myself in the mirror and bless the reflection of my ego and fears, so that these parts of me continue to lose their power over me.

Being in a state of divine light is to let go of ego. Your ego always resists when it is threatened. Remember that if you feel that you must resist this work, refuse to ask for help, or just literally feel like you are not worthy of feeling "better" or whole, this is the frightened and fragile ego in action. It feels that it is losing its control over you! Challenge that fear by continuing to do your best to honor yourself. Do your best to continue the inner work. Challenge the thoughts of self-judgment or the projections that you might have that feel like others are judging you. This is also the voice of fear. Nurture the parts of you that know you are amazing, unique, whole, loving, compassionate, kind, etc., by observing with gratitude and blessings when these *loving* parts are alive and active in you.

Observe your fear with curiosity. I have found that journeying to the Upper World and "watching" myself from this perspective with my spirit guide can be of great assistance. Ask your guide to support you in acknowledging and releasing whatever is keeping you separate from your wholeness, and you might be surprised at the "movie" you might be watching. This is powerful and insightful work. The Universe and your Guides are very interested in assisting you, and when you are motivated from this loving space of doing your own inner work, first and foremost, this is living life fully and with meaning.

This brings us to a *very* important point: our expectations and our attachment to outcomes. We all have expectations. We are taught from when we were very young to have certain expectations for certain behaviors. If we were "good", we might get to stay up a half an hour later at bedtime. If we were "bad" there were unpleasant consequences.

We go through our lives with expectations: if I do well in school, of course, I get good grades. We are constantly being shown that our value comes from somewhere outside of us, for example, through the attainment of gold stars for achievements. This forms a very strong part of our value system, and from what I have noticed, creates a society of people who feel quite entitled. We also learn that our worth comes from external means.

We concentrate on achievements, and constantly compare ourselves to others. If that person has such and such, then I should have the same or better. There is nothing wrong with an intention to do your best, but if it constantly feeds the part of you that is competitive, judgmental, or feeling unequal, you are feeding your fears. So how does this outward perspective of self-valuation affect us while on a shamanic spiritual path?

If we have an attachment to achieving a certain outcome, or that by manipulating another person, even with the best intentions, to effect change in them, we are creating from fear and trying to change our outer circumstances so that we feel better.

This is a very old habit that humanity has been engaged in since time immemorial. It is very clear to me that we must be very cognizant of our intentions before taking action. If we are trying to change our circumstances rather than looking at what is going on within ourselves to see if there is something to be learned or something that needs to change within ourselves to affect our growth, that is not healthy. It does not allow growth or spiritual evolution. It would be so much more compassionate and loving for the course of human consciousness to do the inner work, and find the truth of our own value within us. If we weren't so intent on manipulating others so that they fit our fear-based needs and judging ourselves in various capacities, we would be creating our reality from a much different dream.

You as a whole are more powerful than the sum total of your fears. Sometimes, fear seems like it is all of who we are. Ask your guides to help you through this fearful time, with love and self-compassion. What lessons are you meant to learn from the circumstance that you are creating and experiencing? Sometimes, the lessons are very simple... you are meant to love yourself, no matter what. You are meant to have a life of joy and authenticity, no matter what.

When you are able to look at your life from the perspective of these loving lessons, circumstances tend not to overwhelm or take over. We are really here to learn about loving ourselves, being self-compassionate, and to effect self-empowerment, and by going inward and exploring our divine state of unlimited potential, this is more than possible. If, for example, you find yourself late for work, caught in traffic, and your anger is rising, do your best to go inward. Take a deep breath. This circumstance is here for a reason. What are you going to choose to do?

If your pattern is to get angry, you have a choice in this moment. Are you going to react in the same old way, and curse the traffic, judge yourself for being late, or blame everyone else for your predicament? If you have the presence, and you have been practicing this in the privacy of your own sacred space in your home, take a deep breath. Since you are in your car, it is not appropriate to close your eyes, but you *can* get through this nevertheless. Take another breath and notice what you are feeling in your body.

Ask your guides to assist you in this moment. Ask for clarity with regards to this circumstance. Ask, "What am I meant to learn from this painful experience?" Are you feeling what is going on in your body? Is there discomfort within your body at the thought of being late? How can you express this sense of powerlessness in a healthy way and not send your angry and fearful energy out into the world? Ask your guides to assist you in understanding. They are right there in the car with you. Observe your breathing, and observe the sensations in your body. Ask your guides to assist you in understanding the discomfort that you are feeling. Open to your intuitive ability. Your anger isn't just about the circumstance, and deep down you know this. It is much deeper than your reaction. This is a life pattern that you have perpetuated through fear. Ask your guides to provide clarity on what is keeping you separate from being in your most radiant light in *this* moment. What fear is being triggered right here, right now?

This is the deeper work, and working through these situations in the best way that you can is your life's most important work. To look at these experiences with the intention to heal what is within you is empowering, and is the growth that I keep alluding to.

There are many layers to your fears, and the first opportunity to take to challenge this fear, you may manage to take one conscious breath, and honk the horn right after that breath anyway. But consider this: before this moment, you may have honked the horn in reaction, without even considering one conscious breath. That one breath, with a healing intention, has shifted energy even if it was just ever so slightly. This is growth!

If your old pattern of reacting in anger rises quickly and intensely, just consider how powerfully you have just challenged that anger by taking one breath with intention and consciousness. For that second, you were not spreading more fear into the world. This is great work! Your guides and the Universe want this healing for you, and they are supporting you all the time. You are not alone in this work.

I have also encountered in my practice and through teaching, a few people who desperately think they wanted to learn to live shamanically. They have created their own definition of what living shamanically really means. They wanted to gaze at the stars, travel through the vast cosmos and leave the Earth plane. When working with people who express these dreamlike states of being, and unclear intentions, I ask a lot of questions to gain clarity on what their true intention is. Sometimes these perpetual dreamers, stargazers, or idealists merely want to leave the planet or their unfortunate circumstances, as they see themselves in the moment. They are not happy in their life, and they feel that shamanism is the great escape from that reality. They have just about enough information to be dangerous to themselves.

Some people do not feel happy or hopeful in this reality. They are continuously looking for ways to escape it. Dis-ease has manifested in their bodies through fear-based emotional causes, and they have created dull, lackluster lives, or worse, physical or mental illness. Or they may be thrill seekers, always looking for the next exhilarating sport or dangerous activity. I find that some of these dreamers are the ones who seek out the hallucinogens or medicine plants without a clear intention. They are looking so far outside of themselves for validation, worthiness, excitement or a thrill that they cannot imagine exploring their own inner world in a compassionate or loving way. They imagine their inner world as being as dull and lifeless as they perceive their outward existence, and literally wish to leave this present reality through whatever means available.

These frustrated, frightened people are lost, but think that they have found a way to circumvent the inner work that is required for growth. Perhaps they think that some mind-expanding hallucinogenic drug will save them from feeling the pain of powerlessness that is so present in them, and this shamanic path looks like a legitimate or justifiable way to do that. Perhaps they think that journeying to another reality will take the problems they are encountering in this reality away.

These unhappy people need to actually practice more inner work, and would benefit from working with a shamanic practitioner so that they are being facilitated in a loving way toward a more self-compassionate path. Just as with all of us, they have choice, and they may not choose that path in this lifetime.

I cannot stress enough that to be a true shaman, and to live in a shamanic way, with compassion, self-love, honesty, integrity, respect and reverence, requires continuous inner work. It requires constant diligence in unearthing your fears so you are aware of them, no matter how painful, and having a clear intention to heal what might be lurking below the fear. There is no short cut, and the really amazing healers that have come into my life as teachers, mentors and peers have all done their share of their own personal work. This inner work has made them into the fantastic healers that they are.

The wonderful thing about *life* is that you will be given another opportunity to explore the fearful aspects in you and to explore the choices in the moment, perhaps even before you arrive at work on the same morning as the earlier incident shared above. Talk about the perfection of the Universe! That is compassionate support!

Chapter Seven

I Have So Many Questions – or – Having the Foot on the Gas and the Brake at the Same Time!

Because we have egos and personalities, and are experiencing the human condition, we also have moments of feeling self-conscious. Fundamental feelings of unworthiness assist us in creating self-doubt, keeping us in our thoughts. These thoughts are held in a very limited space – the space of our own mind.

Our brains are a huge gift. They are powerful and allow us to do so much, but they are also a place of dichotomy, separation, limited capacity, polarized thinking, and duality. Within our brain, we create comparison, and because of the brain's hemispheric construction, there is always going to be this sense of black and white, right or wrong, better or worse, and the capacity to judge, arrange, compare and separate all of these dichotomies. This is how we discern. This is how we learn facts and retain knowledge. This is also how we have kept ourselves separate from others throughout history. We constantly compare, and in this comparison, we react to whether we feel we need to know more, or whether we know more than the next guy.

We continually compare and feel unequal to others. Whether we feel inferior or superior is really of little consequence. We will be creating from that point in time in fear: fear that we are not the same; that we are different, and that this is the way that it has to be. We believe that this sense of being different from others means that we are unworthy to be here, or that we are not lovable, or that the other guy is more worthy or more loveable.

If you are reading this book, there is a part of you that has had at least a glimmer, a realization, a light bulb moment, or a dream that there is something more... that somewhere within us, there is something that feels this constant feeling of "something is missing in me", is just not the whole truth! We begin to notice that others are reading the same types of books, listening to the same type of inspirational speakers, and we begin to seek something that might fill this sense of longing within us for understanding and fellowship.

The sense that there is more is *inner knowing*. It is the truth, and many are experiencing more and more of these glimmers, these dreams that are reconnecting us and opening our hearts to the possibilities that might manifest when we shift our consciousness.

The brain, in collusion with fearful parts of us, both of which are so often based in basic fear, litmus tests our every experience. We are very used to listening to this chorus of, "Yah, but did you consider this?" or, "Well others can have peace, but this is not something that I can have!"

When we begin to explore the deeper possibilities and connection that we have with our guides and teachers, your brain, personality and ego are likely to team up in fear trying to talk you out of deeper exploration. I hear many questions from people learning to journey about what they are seeing: is it all in my head? How do I know this is my Guidance? Is this my mind talking? Did I just create this with my imagination?

We really have our doubts, don't we?

I am always interested to hear what people see and don't see in a journey. I love to hear people share their experiences. In a group, there will always be a few who have vivid, colorful, inspiring journeys, and there are always a few who say they got "nothing". There are those who feel they "imagined" the visions in their own minds. How would they know if their journey was the presence of Guidance, or something that they "dreamed up" in their own minds?

One of the first questions that I ask people who feel they are not getting anything, is to describe their experience during the drumming. What did they feel? Most will say that they felt relaxed, but some will feel agitated. Together, we explore the feelings and sensations in their body. Did they have unpleasant sensations, or did it feel pleasant? Did they even notice what was going on in the body, or were they fixated on the thoughts in their head? These are not judgments on my part, but a way to begin to bring understanding around being present and open, and engaged in the moment. This takes practice.

After that discussion, which will usually glean some insights into their level of presence and their understanding of practicing with openness, and without self-judgment, we can delve a little deeper. Did they hear anything? Did they smell anything? Did they feel anything around them? Sometimes, we are so resistant, distracted or just plain stubborn that we choose not to see the positive aspects of our journey. Maybe you didn't have a conversation with Einstein while visiting the Upper World, but even with your blindfold on, did you sense a brighter light in this realm? Did it seem darker, or thicker? Did you feel hotter or colder?

We were given these bodies for a reason, and the sensations that we are able to feel are all part of it. Again, this work is going to support you in really understanding your vehicle (body) as it relates to your life lessons here on the Earth plane. Perhaps one of the messages from your Guidance is to recognize when you are relaxed, and how it feels to trust that you are safe in the moment. Our guides generally attempt to give us messages in a way that we will understand them. If, for some reason, we ignore or don't catch this message, Guidance will find a way to repeat the message, often within a day or two.

We don't know the lesson plan that the Universe has in store for us, nor can we grow spiritually until we experience, feel and move through the lessons with presence, intention and commitment.

If you continually "get lost" or are becoming increasingly

frustrated about your journeys, try chanting your journey out loud. Using a rattle or drum, or a drumming CD, sing or chant your journey. In the privacy of your own sacred space, state your intention and then describe your journey *out loud*, for example:

Example of chanting a journey:

I travel down the roots of my favorite tree, and I feel the warmth of the dirt around me. I smell the earth and I feel myself falling down, down, down toward the Lower World. I feel my stomach churning slightly as I fall down through the roots of my tree. I am traveling to the Lower World to talk with my spirit helper, to ask her to guide me in finding a resolution in the conflict I have with my co-worker, Tom. I am seeking Guidance for resolution on this issue. I feel myself reach a dark tunnel and I continue going down, down, down. I feel the tunnel shifting, and I sense myself walking on level ground, and up ahead I see a light. I see the light that leads me to the place where I will meet My Helping Spirit (You can name or describe your helper, too).

I walk slowly and steadily, and I see the light coming closer to me. I feel the warmth of the tunnel and I feel myself becoming excited to see my friend again! I intend to ask her how to resolve a conflict with my co-worker Tom. I walk into the light, and see that I am in a familiar meadow. I see the sky above me, and I see that there is a huge tree in the middle of the meadow. I know that I need to move toward this tree and I am walking quickly now. I know that I will meet my Helper there.

I feel my feet walking on the path, and the breeze on my skin. I love to walk in this fresh air, and I love to meet my friend. I am excited to speak with her to resolve my conflict with Tom at work. I hear my power animal just ahead of where I am walking and I am grateful to acknowledge her presence. We smile at each other, and hug like old friends. I ask her the question that I have come here for: "How do I resolve the conflict with my co-worker, Tom?" She looks at me and smiles knowingly, and I am open to receive her response....

Keep chanting and singing. As you await an answer, keep repeating your intention and remind your power animal or teacher that you are open to receiving the answer. Once received, thank your Guide, and chant your journey back the way that you came, describing how you feel, and describing the path that you take back to your starting point.

It doesn't matter what tune or rhythm or pace happens to evolve. It doesn't matter what your voice sounds like. It doesn't matter if you feel stuck, or forget where you are going. If you find yourself "stuck" just repeat the last phrase you chanted again, or restate your intention and you will find your way again. I love leading journeys this way, as it is very helpful for those who have any issues with focus, for example, some beginners with strong resistance, or clients with ADD or ADHD. I chant or sing the journey for them, and it has been very helpful to them to join me, to journey alongside me. Interestingly enough, they will encounter their own Guidance, often taking a side trip of their own, but they are able to find their way back to my voice when they are ready to return.

You might also find that a CD of a guided journey would be helpful. I can highly recommend a CD by Sandra Ingerman, called Shamanic Meditations. On this CD, she guides the participant through several wonderful experiences.

Just as with life, there are "good" days and "bad" days to journey. Perhaps I should say that there are some less than optimum days to journey, and this is all part of a very natural cycle. We must remember that our society, our jobs, and our own limiting beliefs feel that we need to be successful, perfect, and strong every day. This is certainly not the way of nature. Look at the cycles around you. In the spring, we tend to feel rejuvenated. There is increasing light compared to the dark winter. The plants that have been resting over the winter start their growth cycle again. We in the northern hemisphere tend to be more active and outdoors in the spring and summer months, as the fall and winter can be very cold. Plants and trees don't bloom all year.

When a member of the tribe who requires a healing visits the shaman of the village, it is not unheard of for the client to be turned away as the shaman felt it was not a good day to journey.

My own patterns and cycles are pretty predictable: I am more active and energized in the transitional seasons. I feel particularly productive in the fall, which may stem back to my excitement each year about going back to school. It is like the beginning of the year for me! So I tend to be much more focused and disciplined in my rituals and feel more connected during the fall, even though I do know that winter will follow. What happens for me in the winter is that I become more reflective. This is when I spend more time indoors, and I write or jot down ideas about future plans for workshops. I find that I am able to journey longer and perhaps more deeply in the winter. I also know that I am not a morning person, so I never schedule clients before ten o'clock in the morning. Recognize your own patterns of productiveness with honesty.

I also know that when I am working with a client, or even when I am in ritual for myself, there are going to be days when I am less insightful, or that I don't seem to have the clarity that I have at other times. This is normal, and I have learned not to get frustrated by the times when I don't have the clarity or insight of my more productive cycles. I know that they will return.

Please do not get discouraged if your journeys are not what you expect. Remember, we have so much attachment to things being a certain way, and we expect so much from ourselves. This work is about creating an intimate relationship with your Guidance, so that you can challenge your deepest fears, answer your most important questions and have the life that you were meant to live. This work is meant to set you free from your negative thoughts, your limiting beliefs, and become aware of whatever is keeping you separate from being your most radiant and precious self.

You might be asking yourself, for what intentions should I journey?

Really, there are *no* questions for which you cannot journey to seek Guidance. Once you have become comfortable in allowing yourself to be transported to Non-Ordinary Reality, you can trust your guides to take you to the most appropriate place for learning. This is your own personal library of learning, and the wisdom is infinite. Try not to over think it!

What questions have come up for you? Perhaps, even while journeying, you have been given some images or messages that do not make sense to you at the time. Journey again and ask for the meaning of the images. What was the message that was being conveyed to you? Ask for meaning in a way that you will understand it.

In your daily life, you might have realized that your circumstances were offering a lesson for you. More often than not, we get so wrapped up in the circumstance that we are unable to perceive the lesson being conveyed. Journey and ask your Guidance what you are meant to learn by this situation.

Consider the following intentions, and don't limit your imagination. There is no doubt that more ideas and questions will come up over time.

- Perhaps you are having some health issues. Journey to ask how best to support healing of your physical body.
- Do you wish to explore the mysteries of your life? What was the reason that you incarnated in this lifetime? What is your purpose here in the Earth School?
- You can always speak with deceased relatives or other loved ones, to say what you may not have been able to tell them while they were here in physical form.
- If you have a conflict with a living person, journey to ask for ways to resolve this.

- Create a deeper relationship with the natural world. If you live in an urban setting, what does it feel like to be a tree? What does a river feel like? What does a mountain experience?
- Interpretation of dreams is a very popular intention for journeying. I have found that when I wake up from a particularly confusing dream, it is really beneficial to ask for guidance, especially while it is fresh in my mind. I have also found that I have been able to finish a dream that might have been interrupted by a late night phone call or midnight storm. Incredibly, I have also been able to change the ending of a disturbing dream by asking my helping spirits for a more gentle way to receive my messages, and re-entered the dream to have an alternate or more enlightening ending.
- Perhaps there is a situation at work that needs attention. Ask for Guidance on how to restore peace in that environment.
- Ask your guides what you should journey for next.
- Perhaps you need help creating a ceremony for yourself to deepen your connection with your dreams and desires, and how to manifest them.

Is your reluctance or confusion surrounding finding the intention for a journey due to having your foot on the accelerator and the brake at the same time? Are you coasting, with no particular course in mind? You are the driver. Take the car out of neutral. Trust in your imagination, and experiment with setting the GPS – Guidance, personally speaking.

There is no end to the journey, just like your life, although physically finite on this Earth plane, the energetic and spirit world is infinite! Journey to explore the aspects of this spirit world in Non-Ordinary Reality. Perhaps you will come across other helping spirits who will assist you with specific questions. This is a wonderful new world for exploring. Enjoy yourself!

Chapter Eight

The Tools of the Trade – or – Where is the Spare Tire?

I hope that you are enjoying your self-exploration, and that the guides are showing you many exciting and wonderful things in your journeys! These explorations can be healing journeys, and initiations. I hope that you are benefitting from them by remembering that you are whole, precious and loved by the Universe! I trust that you are having glimpses of your importance in the Universe, and that you are beginning to sense your connection with all things on Earth and in the Cosmos!

In deepening our personal practice, we are sometimes guided by spirit to have our own sacred drum and rattle. As you have experienced in journeying, the drum is a sonic driver, creating the theta state of brainwaves that allow you to travel into Non-Ordinary Reality. Rattles can be used for the same purpose, but also offer a powerful way to open sacred space, connecting and speaking to the helping spirits, drawing them closer to you.

Perhaps you have been moved or guided to find or make a rattle or a drum. I have experienced journeys in my own personal life where I have been told the exact color, the sound, the size, and the method with which to construct these sacred items. Perhaps you have had these journeys or have somehow heard the sound of your drum or rattle in your dreams.

I love to experiment with sounds! Before the drums and rattles that I use now came to me, I experimented with some interesting things. I used bottles of aspirin, or bottles filled with corn or course sand, and found their sounds to be quite transformative. I also used tiny boxes with tiny rocks or gemstones in them. Many of these simple tools worked very well, and I suggest that you try things from your kitchen, pantry, or bathroom. A jar of Himalayan bath salts was quite a powerful rattle for me at one time. I have had some very insightful journeys with containers of whole black pepper or wild rice.

To be an instrument of transformation, your rattle needs to sound "right" for you. I have seen some very beautiful and expensive rattles that weren't appropriate for my journeying, but were perfect for someone else. It is important for you to *feel* the sound and allow it to take you where you need to go! Any rattle, fancy or not, can be a beautiful helper for you.

Recently, I was waiting for my drink at a local coffee shop. I was patiently sitting and reading the paper when I realized that there was a beautiful rattling sound near me. Imagine my joy at seeing a beautiful youngster sitting in her stroller, rattling away with a colorful plastic rattle. The sound of this rattle was rich and the smile on the little one's face was filled with ecstasy. I couldn't help but remember that my daughter had a beautiful rattle when she was a baby. How soon we forget the transformative qualities and magic that these simple toys contain. This tiny person in the coffee shop with her glowing face and beautiful rattle was a very strong reminder that I don't have to have something ornate, fancy or expensive for this work. It was all about the wonderful sound and energy of this simple tool.

You might be drawn or guided to make a rattle from rawhide, shell, animal hoof, antler, or a gourd. There are all sorts of raw materials that have been used for the construction of rattles by indigenous people around the world. Perhaps in our modern world, a thought to recycling might offer a green alternative for materials for these wonderful tools. Recycling a child's toy, or reusing a favorite bottle or box might be the fodder for your new rattle.

This is exciting and sacred work, and I encourage you to be reverent and filled with gratitude to your Guidance if this experience enfolds for you. Your guides will assist you in the actual construction of your rattle, and the materials will be given to you in a most magical way, I am sure. When I was guided to make a rattle, it was with speed and synchronicity that I was invited to a Native craft class within days of the journey where my helping spirit offered this guidance. Since that time, I have also been gifted other kinds and types of rattles. One even looks like a rock, but is a hollow clay "rock" that has tiny stones inside it. It is a beautiful tool. Some rattles that I have found sound like bells, and their distinct music has a very special purpose in my work. All rattles have their own wonderful qualities and tones. In my healing practice, different rattles assist in different types of work. Some are loud and somewhat aggressive, others are soft and gentle. Some rattles help me call in the helping spirits, some spirit away energy that is no longer required. Some say thank you, some say welcome home and others say goodbye. They are all wonderful gifts.

A drum is a very special shamanic tool. If you are journeying to a drumming CD, you are probably aware of its wonderful ability to transport you to an altered state of reality. My first experience with a drumming meditation many years ago changed my life! I was very used to meditation with soft music and relaxation, and yogic meditation with quieting the mind in silence and opening to wisdom. Once I journeyed to the sound of a drum, I no longer felt the deep relaxation nor could I partic-ipate in this type of meditation in a passive way. My first experience with a shaman drumming, took me immediately into the vast cosmos, spiraling wildly in space, seeing pictures, feeling excited, and having fun. This was one of those moments when I understood that this experience was something I wanted more of. This was a meditation where I was not tempted to sleep, and I was participating fully and actively in the journey.

I generally find that if people have a tendency to fall asleep during a meditation, they don't have that experience during drumming. In all the years that I have supported people through shamanic practices, I have had two people fall asleep during a drumming journey. I was drumming for myself, and journeying on behalf of these two clients. They were able to relax their mind enough and allow the healing session to just wash over them as they slept. It was a gift for both of them, as their usual resistance to healing was not active during this sleepy session. Really, it is not a problem if you do fall asleep during a session, as you will have the experience you are meant to in any case! I do find that it is much less likely that you will drift off if you are drumming for yourself, however.

There are as many drums out there as there are people, and some are very expensive. Again, before I acquired my first drum, I experimented with sounds. I drummed on boxes made of cardboard and wood. I drummed on the floor. I drummed on my massage table. Some of these drums were very effective.

Again, I was very fortunate to make a drum of rawhide in the very timely native craft class in which I made my rattle. Although I still use this drum today, I have some particular challenges with drums that are made of animal skin. It was not so much an ethical quandary about the skin itself, as the hide for my drum was taken from an animal during a ceremony, and was prayed for and used with reverence, however, I do find that the natural hide drums are sometimes difficult to maintain. They do change in sound and tone, depending on the amount of humidity in the environment. Where I live, the weather can change very quickly, and I have found that the drum I love when it is dry and clear outside gets loose and dull when the weather is rainy. Traveling to other countries can be difficult for this reason, and also because some jurisdictions have strict rules regarding natural skins. Therefore, I have chosen for my usual daily use, and when I travel, a Remo synthetic drum. These drums are a man-made material, which is not affected by temperature or moisture. They are incredibly durable, and lightweight to carry while drumming or traveling.

Choose a drum that sounds "right" for you. Even in the store, you will sense or feel when you hear the perfect drum sound for you. Your heart may jump, or you will sense emotion rising in your body. You will establish a relationship with this tool, which begins when you meet. When you play "your" drum, notice what responses you have in your body. You will know immediately if the sound of this special instrument speaks to you. Indigenous people around the world have made reference to the beat of a drum, comparing it to the heart of Mother Earth, and connecting our heartbeats to hers.

I have a very good friend who knew that she was being guided in her journeys to have her own drum. She was often traveling to a small area in southern Alberta when a native craft store caught her eye. She stopped in and tried some drums, but none seemed to really resonate with her. One afternoon, after dropping in on a number of previous occasions, she stopped by one more time. A beautiful dark-skinned drum caught her eye, and as she sat down, placed the drum gently in her left hand, and ran her right hand over it, tears formed in her eyes. She knew she had found her sacred companion.

A drum can become your voice. You may release emotion through it. It speaks for you and to you. It is an incredible friend and can assist you by expressing things that you want to say through this magnificent living being, because it does live. You will see what I mean when you find your true companion.

You may wish to paint the surface or embellish your drum with ribbons around the edge, or hang beads or feathers on it. This is your drum, and you will be guided to its personalization. Make it yours.

I have only one word of caution... drums tend to be rather loud, so be considerate of your neighbors!

Chapter Nine

Where to Now? – or –
What is Around The Next Bend?

You are probably getting to know your guides and helping spirits very well by now. I know that they will continue to provide important information for you to continue on your journey of connection to Nature's spirits, and the expansion of your consciousness.

One of my early concerns and a part of me that tries to distract me and keep me from being my most radiant light is a fear that I am not very creative. I read many books and took lots of courses to continue growing spiritually by identifying and challenging these fears within me. However, the intention for this obsessive reading and learning was fear based. I thought that if I read enough, studied enough or learned enough, this would make up for my lack of creative ability. How interesting are the voices of our fears! When I journeyed, I would ask my helping spirits to help me be more creative, and they would often laugh at me, or show me some very amusing scene from my life. My helping spirits have an amazing sense of humor, but at first, I thought they were laughing at me. I have had many conversations with them to that effect.

Our helping spirits love to assist us. What mine remind me about constantly is that I am often far too serious, too studious, and way too fearful that I might be lacking in creative expression, so they show me, with humor, how I might do things differently. I am so grateful that they support me. I still sometimes wish they didn't seem so flippant, however, their attitude does remind me to laugh at my own fears, effectively cutting them down to size.

When do I journey? I journey when I need insight. I journey when I am creating workshops or classes. I journey before I see a new client, to see how I might best be of service to them. I journey when I am writing. I journey when I need insight into a health concern or question about myself or another person. I journey when I need an answer about a relationship with a friend or loved one. I journey when I need direction. I enjoy journeying, and have learned that I don't need to struggle with an issue, question or problem by myself. I have helpers available to me all the time. I never feel alone, even though I work at home a lot, and may only see one or two people a day. I can consult my Guidance at any time, day or night, and this assists me in knowing that I am personally guided. I am still in awe of the level of support that I can receive from my beautiful and wise helpers, and I sense and feel the love that they have for me.

All of this has very much helped me along my healing path. I have tended all my life to be very self-judgmental and self critical, but I am feeling the shifts within me as I gain self-acceptance, and compassion. This is truly a path of healing and expansion. I have constructed and nurture a more loving and compassionate perspective of myself, and this has assisted me in sharing the gifts that I have to share with others. I support many people in their own healing, facilitate workshops and classes, and constantly learn about myself as I grow and change. I feel excited and positive about the future of human existence, as so many people seem interested in healing themselves and the planet on which they live.

So where do *you* wish to go next? If you are having even the tiniest glimpses or insights about the changes that you are creating and experiencing, while working with your loving guides and teachers, and creating your life in a different way, where can this work take you? I suggest that you and your guides can go anywhere! If you had told me ten years ago while I was managing an accounting group in an oil and gas company that I would be standing in a circle of people, whistling, chanting, drumming, and rattling, I would have probably laughed out loud. But here I am. That is precisely what I am often doing. And I love it!

I think one of the most amazing parts of this journey is the reverence that I feel for all life, beginning with my own self. I sense the expansiveness that I continually feel in my heart, and I am filled with a sense of unlimited possibility, hope and purpose. I honor this process, Mother Earth and the Universe for the growth and healing that I am experiencing, and the assistance that I can provide for others. I understand that as I allow my own light and potential to be my truth and reality, and as I radiate my most brilliant light, this supports healing in the world.

How does one remember to radiate their light? This is such a deep question, but it is of utmost importance. This is the rubber meeting the road. This is where the meaning is. As I begin to consider my preciousness, and nurture the loving qualities that I possess I begin to affect the world in a positive way. This requires my being compassionate first with *myself.*

As you continue to gift yourself with love in meditation and journeying every day, you will begin to feel your love as the precious gift that it is. By giving yourself that time every day, as we talked about earlier, you honor your preciousness. You will deepen your relationship with all that is natural in the world, even if you live on the thirtieth floor of a high rise. I know many shamanic practitioners who work in large cities, but are using their creativity, imagination, and intention for healing in amazing ways in support of their clients. And you can do this for yourself.

To deepen your reverence and connection with self, may I suggest asking your helping spirits to give you your own sacred song? In your journeying, you will begin to hear a series of notes or tones that will resonate with you. This is a powerful affirmation of your existence, your uniqueness, and your self-compassion. We are all worthy of a song, and this one will be created just for you.

Journey to your helping spirits and ask them for your sacred song. Perhaps this will mean that several of your helpers will work together, or perhaps one of them will escort you to a very special place, or to a new guide specifically for this purpose. I have journeyed to a crystal cave of music and sound to retrieve these special songs for clients and for myself. Your guides will show you the way, and you will be given a song for you. Have a digital recorder handy as you begin to sing your song. Sometimes cell phones have the capability for recording. Just be sure to turn off the cell network, so that your phone ringing will not disturb you.

Once you receive your sacred song, sing it often. Don't worry, judge or think you did something wrong if your song is actually whistling, or even a particular rhythm on the drum or a pattern of rattling. Listen to your Guidance. Whatever the song, it is meaningful for you on a soul level. Allow yourself to feel what this song brings up for you.

Sounds are very powerful. I love working with crystal bowls and chimes. I also use my voice in healing sessions when I am guided to do so. Never discount the power of your voice or the vibration from your drum or the significance of a chime or bell. I sing the sacred song that was given to me in a journey to open sacred space before a ceremony, workshop or at the beginning of every client's shamanic sessions. I will speak about opening space in just a little while.

By singing these few notes with presence, reverence and groundedness, I remember my own wholeness, and open myself fully to my guides and teachers. It helps me let go of any egoistic thoughts, and I focus completely on the work at hand. It is a way for me to thank my guides upfront for the support that I know I will receive.

As I alluded to earlier when I talked about the hollow bones, movement is also a way to shake off ego, fear or limiting beliefs. As a healer, I dance to clear myself fairly regularly. My clearing dance is called a bone dance. I move to the drumming or rattling, until my ego is gone, and I am just the hollow bones that are open conduits for healing energy. Movement is a great way to let go of things that no longer serve you. It is also a very powerful way to integrate things that have been shared with you by your Guidance.

Dance like no one is watching! Dance to your sacred soul song, or dance while you drum or rattle for yourself. Dance to a fantastic piece of music that allows you to feel free. Dance to the rhythm of the wind or the rain. Movements like this are the way the ancestors honored their Mother, the Earth, and their Father, the Sky. They danced in community to empower the tribe. Perhaps some ancient wisdom will be imparted to you through dance.

To honor your power animal and the wisdom he shares with you, dance the movements and emotions, the strengths and attitudes of your power animal. This can be really fun and empowering as you embody the attributes and support of the animal that loves you. Put on your drumming CD, or grab a rattle or drum, and dance the movements of your animal. If it flies, open your wings. If it roars, roar. If it swims, move through the room like you are swimming. This is a phenomenal bonding exercise with your spirit friend and helper. I would carefully remind you that you are not allowing your power animal to take you over or possess you. You are merging with him, but *you* are in control of the dance. You can reflect, feel, and emulate his energy, but he does not overtake you in any way.

Another great way to express yourself creatively is to draw or write. Draw a picture of a vision received in a journey, and when revisiting this drawing, deepen the understanding of the journey, or gain clarity around it with a different perspective. The drawing will likely elicit a physical response in the body. Take some time to be with that sensation, gleaning more meaning or a different interpretation of the picture. Experiment with drawing and/or writing about your journeys, as this diary of visual reminders, or words, is a powerful way to honor yourself through creative expression. These are important visions or key phrases surrounding emotions that can clear your way to much understanding.

Journeying is a profound way of divining truth and learning about the meaning of certain situations, people who are in your life, and about yourself. Divination journeying is performed through specific intention, and through this strong intention, consider drawing any pictures, visions, symbols or images that you see during these journeys. Drawing is a profound tool for "connecting the dots". These types of journeys, where we have asked something about a future event or are divining information to support potential choices, often give images or fragments of visions. Repeatedly going on a similar intended journey of divination, and keeping all the pictures that were drawn afterward, the whole picture will often reveal its meaning.

Never give up when asking for information. Sometimes your patience might be being tested. The answer is always worth waiting for, and it appears not only when it is time, but also when we allow it. Through journeying, and deepening our relationship with Spirit, we can put a jigsaw puzzle of images together to complete the picture and its message.

During a journey, a particular theme or repetitive image may come up for consideration. Remember that your spirit helpers generally give messages in metaphors. It is fascinating to me that when we return to this reality, we will often start to see these images in things around us. For instance, I have journeyed to ask my guides about an idea for a topic for my journeying class. In my journey, I might have seen various flowers of many colors, shapes and sizes. I know that it is not usually meant that I should literally place flowers around the room, so I open myself to what this might mean in a more metaphoric sense. I might smell the fragrant flowers or begin to see more flowers of a similar type.

What type are these flowers? Heart shapes may appear, or I see more roses than other types of flowers.

Now I am getting somewhere! I know what roses mean for me – love, heartfelt joy and relationship. Then I ask other questions – how do these words fit into the question that I am asking and the Guidance that I am being given? I might see couples walking together, hand in hand, or recognize a couple that I know, which then gives me more ideas. Suddenly the theme is beginning to form. Should I invite couples, or those seeking a life partner? I get more Guidance. I might see the same couple that I know, indicating that it might be a couples' class that I should create, and then I can ask for more clarity around that. It is all given in a way that I understand, and in the way that I can visualize images and therefore create.

I might go for a walk. My helping spirits always walk with me, and I can surely deepen my understanding by setting the intention to make this walk an *omen walk*. I will be open to what nature, through the outdoor walk, has to share with me. I look with awareness for signs. I might see a pair of hawks flying in the sky, or a pair of gophers. Certain animals mean certain things for me. For example, my adopted Nakoda brother reminds me constantly about the magpie, which is a powerful messenger. I am particularly aware when I notice a number of magpies flying in front of me. What should I think if I see a coyote? My brother tells me to be wary of what I am thinking, because the coyote often tries to trick us. Coyote is a great reminder that there is more than one way to look at a question or problem.

I might see a heart-shaped rock or other omen to indicate that I am on the right track in my thinking. Then again, I might see two branches forming an X, which might mean to dig a little deeper with my helpers to consider a different perspective. This is what being open is all about; being flexible and allowing whatever wisdom is available to be allowed into my awareness. I cannot be rigid in my thinking or righteous about my ideas being the only correct ones. Again, I have so much support if my ego and I get out of the way.

I find incredible answers in the skies. I observe the shapes of clouds, and the stories that these shapes may be offering. When looking at photographs of the sky, or of sunsets or sunrises, I will often see the shape of an animal or other messenger within the beauty of the picture.

Omen walks are a great way to deepen understanding, or divine answers or guidance. These walks, which are initiated with clear intention, are a great way to practice trust. And don't think that just because you don't have a natural spot to walk in, you can't do this. Of course, nature walks are very informative and are wonderfully healthy, by assisting in clearing the mind, and breathing fresh air, but I have also had some amazing insights and ideas come up in a mall or when walking downtown.

Do you wonder why your eye keeps getting drawn to a certain book in every bookstore that you pass? Could this be your spiritual helper trying to get your attention? Do you think that is a coincidence? It might not be that you are meant to buy the actual book, but what is the title? Does it have anything to do with what you are asking for on this omen walk (because you would have certainly set an intention for the walk, right)? What about the picture or image on the cover? What about the author's name? For example, perhaps you were asking for clarity about a vacation that you wish to take, and the author's last name is England?

It is fascinating when we stop to look at all the clues we are given along the way. It is so amazing that we have this incredible level of support available to us, and we are often too busy or "mind-full" to notice!

You don't even need to be out walking to have these experiences. If you are driving to work with a question on your mind, notice the license plate of the car in front of you as you ponder your issue or question. Does it contain a message? What is the make or color of the vehicle next to you? What song is playing on your radio? Is there a billboard with a message just for you? Did you notice a bird flying across your path? This is a great opportunity to be present with awareness and openness, and you are literally in the driver's seat.

It is also possible to have these omens and signs offered to you when you are watching TV or a movie. Open yourself to what is going on behind the scenes, or the background music playing, or the names of the characters. I have received some powerful insights when I have been watching a show in my most aware state.

The omens present in your journeys, your walks, and your drives are specifically tailored for your learning, and are in a language of metaphors that are meaningful just for you. Notice any repetitive messages, which may bring clarity or make sense as you string the patterns of the messages together.

Chapter Ten

Creating Sacred Space – or – I'm Cleaning out the Car for Passengers!

This work is sacred, and demands your full attention with reverence, compassion and care. For me, I feel that the more I know about the possibilities for healing, and the potential power of this work, the more I hold it in respect and reverence. This attention is the least that I can do to honor the guidance and support that I know is being given to me, as, with their help and assistance, the co-creation of life through my intentions and dreams becomes reality.

I feel that to create an atmosphere of sacredness for the work, as I expand and deepen my intentions and the purpose of my work, it is my responsibility to be engaged 100 percent, as present as possible and open to the limitless potential in the moment. This is true for driving my car as well – I should be 100 percent engaged and paying attention to the road. I also want to acknowledge the whole team of helping spirits that assist me in the process.

As we have discussed, the creation of an altar and/or a sacred place within your home is a very key element of respect for the work. This place within your personal environment highlights the value you place on your inner work. It places the sacredness for which you hold your meeting place for Guidance in a different light than any other space in your home. I feel specifically creating this space for rituals and celebrations offers an air of importance and sacredness for how you will honor yourself and your helping spirits, as opposed to where you watch TV, where you cook your meals, or even where you read, although it may be in the same location in your home. The difference will be in your intention and the preparation of the space in the moments that you set aside for your healing rituals or ceremonies.

Many aboriginal people or shamanic practitioners call the preparation of your space *creating sacred space*, or *opening the space*. It pertains to setting the stage, if you will, for the sacredness, the preciousness, and the importance of the blessed gift you are creating for yourself in the moment. I offer these suggestions for the deeper work that you will be doing, but once you understand and feel the difference in energy when you take the time to open the space in this manner, I feel you will be doing this in some form for whatever you wish to do shamanically. I create sacred space each time I sit at the computer to write, for instance. I smudge myself and open space when I am creating workshops, or when I am settling in to journey for myself or for clients. I create sacred space during the beginning of every healing session, every ceremony that I host, and for every sacred event that I participate in. Now that you are doing more, under-standing more, and feeling more, I'm sure that you will feel that you can use this sacred invocation to open space whenever you are journeying or celebrating, too.

From what I have been formally taught, which is primarily through the practices of the First Nations of Western Canada, along with the contemporary teachings I have been exposed to, some Incan and Mayan traditions, and also through journeying to my ancestors for guidance, I have been given the following as the basic format to create sacred space. You may be given, or will be taught or guided to make changes to this, and that is perfectly appropriate. This is an exercise for you, and your helping spirits will assist you in making this particular practice perfect for your purposes. It may reawaken some ancient wisdom held in your DNA. Notice what resonates with you, and perhaps in your dreamtime, or through shamanic journeying, other ancestral prayers or blessings will be given to you for your use.

One critical difference in opening space is a matter of belief and teachings, and that is that some people *invite* or *call in* the helping spirits, and the others you will be working with. Other shamans, practitioners or participants will invoke inspiration or spirit by *decree*. This is typically what I do, thanking the helping spirits and showing my gratitude for the presence of these guides and teachers, as I believe that I am surrounded by their presence all the time. I am setting a predetermined intention for the work to follow, and I welcome their inspiration, guidance and assistance. I do trust that they are there. I am opening my heart, and the hearts of those present at the event to the support that will be offered by our honored guests. I also know that from the perspective of a being a spirit of Divine Light, which I am, and you are too, that these guests are all equal to me... Divine Lights similar to my own. Ask your own Guidance if you need to invite the helping spirits in, or if you, like me, trust that they are there. Neither method is more correct than the other. Listen to your inner voice, and you will know which is more appropriate for you.

The ritual below is how I open space. Of course, the first step is to be clear in my intention, as this will be stated during the invocation. Invocation is more empowering if said out loud, with authority and confidence in your voice, and trusting in your intention. Again, these are the words I typically use, with minor shifts or alterations every time I perform it, as I do not read a script. It comes out the way it comes out. When you open space, you will feel, sense or know what changes are appropriate and necessary for you.

Invocation to open space
*Welcome. Welcome to this ceremony. Tonight, it is my honor to lead this ceremony whose intention is to (**state intention**). I open this space to inspiration. To allowing healing and openness within ourselves (or the singular **myself** in all the following contexts if I am in ritualistic ceremony on my own) to all the wisdom, insight*

and empowerment that is available to us from the Guiding Lights, helping spirits and teachers that we know and the ones we are yet to meet. I acknowledge the Ascended Masters, the Ancestors, the Standing People, the Hidden Folk, the elements, the power of the four directions, the power animals and all the magical people who support and assist us in our work.

I begin by whistling, to bring these spirits closer to our circle, to our fire, and welcome their presence among us. I whistle four times, with reverence, as I sense their energy coming closer. I take a few deep, cleansing breaths, and then begin to rattle. I could drum if I wish, and would be more likely to do that when I am on my own, as there is not a group that also needs to hear the invocation. I find as a facilitator or host, I generally rattle. There is also a traditional belief I hold that the rattle as a shamanic tool brings the spirits in more closely. The sound of the rattle draws them nearer.

Welcome Spirits of the East, where the sun comes up and the day begins. We welcome your presence and your reminder of the beginning of new opportunities present in every moment.

Welcome to the Spirit of the South, who send us the winds of change. Change is our only constant, and you remind us that we can be flexible. We can effect change only for ourselves as we grow and learn.

Spirits of the West, where the sun goes down, and the day ends, thank you for your reminder that with each transition, there must be a death: every beginning has an end: that there is newness and opportunity offered in each moment that we are willing to release old and limited beliefs. Thank you for your presence.

Spirits of the North, where the ancestors live in the Northern Lights, we feel and sense your wisdom, your compassion, and we are grateful that you are here to share with us. Thank you for your loving support.

Spirits of This Land, thank you for letting us sit upon you, work upon you, and be upon you. You have seen all the history, know all the stories of those who have gone before, and you support us by sharing your wisdom with us. Thank you for allowing us to sit with you.

Spirits of the Elements: Air, you allow inspiration to flow into our bodies through our breath. Water, you sustain us and remind us about ease in flowing gently with the current, and in seeing our resistance if we swim against the flow. Fire: you are the light that guides us and warms our hearts. Earth: You are our foundation, our source of grounding. Thank you for your compassionate support.

Spirit of Mother Earth, you support all Life, and we are grateful to you. You share with us your nurturing, your loving spirit and your Guidance. Father Sky, we are in awe of the beauty and vastness of your being. Thank you for being in our circle.

To all the Angels, Hidden Folk, the Standing Folk, the Ascended Masters, the helping spirits and power animals that we know, and those we are yet to meet, and the spirits that I may have forgotten to name, I express my gratitude for your presence here.

Creator, Great Spirit, Great Mystery, we feel you walk with us. We are grateful for your loving Guidance. We do our best to live by your powerful words: "As above, so below. As within, so without." So be it. And so it is. It is done. Today we are together to (state intention), and we are grateful for your presence. We are open to your Guidance. We are blessed by your wisdom.

I sing my own sacred song now, the one given to me in a journey by my guides. I smudge the group and myself, or just myself if I am working alone. I generally light sage, cedar or sweet grass placed in a shell and smudge using a feather if working in a group, or with my hands if I am cleansing myself. I silently invite the smoke to take the intentions, prayers and blessing directly to the Creator. If I have had an insight that the smoke is not going to be appropriate, for instance if there are participants with

allergies in the group, I use a spray of essential oil of the afore-
mentioned sacred plants, or Florida water, as is the tradition in
many South American countries.

If comparing one shamanic culture to another, the ritual of
opening space might be slightly different, but the intention is the
same: to open the space allowing for the participation of all the
helping spirits, to gain permission from the Spirits of the Land to
perform the ceremony, and to create an environment of love,
compassion, reverence, healing and equanimity to support the
specific intention for the ceremony being performed.

The cultural differences may include the use of a rattle versus
a drum. They may use a bone whistle rather than the lips. In
some cultures, all of the spirits of the directions are not always
invoked, as some cultures do not recognize all the directions.
Most shamans agree, however, that the verbal invocation, said
out loud, is more powerful than invoking within the mind, as the
outward use of the voice is expressing the true intentions of the
heart with confidence, authority, reverence and directness.
Within our minds, intentions can become muddied in distraction
or resistance that is not necessarily noticed unless we are saying
it out loud. We might not even realize that we are lost in thought,
if we are not listening to our words said out loud for all to hear. I
believe that the spirits hear my voice and are clear about what I
am asking for when I have the courage to say it out loud.

I also feel that by saying the invocation out loud, I am clear
about my responsibility in the ceremony and indeed in this
lifetime. I am responsible for my own growth, and integrating the
wisdom that I receive from my Guidance is my choice. I choose
to be bold enough to take this responsibility as my own and do
my best not to disempower myself by any means for which I may
be unaware. By saying out loud what I am intending to invoke,
by opening to the Guidance that I am in the presence of, I
genuinely feel the increased strength of my commitment to

myself and to the connection of all of my helping spirits. I feel this when I am saying the words. It is not something that I do by rote... I feel the energies around me, and am genuinely grateful for their presence with me.

Chapter Eleven

More Cycles, More Work?
– or – More Hills to Climb?

As you continue to explore living shamanically, you will be finding more and more ways to honor yourself and the natural world, and deepening your connection with these powerful allies, the natural elements and beings. I am sure that you have been honoring the cyclic nature of your day with more awareness and understanding, sensing and feeling your affinity with the moon cycles. I trust that you are feeling and sensing the changes that this recalibration of your being is creating in your physical body and affecting your outlook on your life. I also know that as I honored these changes within myself, my curiosity grew and I was open to understanding more about our natural world.

All of nature is cyclical and, as we have discussed, there is a lot happening in the natural world, no matter what the time of year. We are identical to the natural world, as we have seasons of growth, seasons of transition, seasons of activity and seasons of reflection that we can learn from with gratitude and thankfulness.

In my spiritual shamanic practice, I maintain and deepen my connection with the spirits and the natural world by honoring *all* the cycles. I host community events to honor the solstices and equinoxes, as I feel it is important to recognize, acknowledge, feel and sense the changes in energy, support these events in the natural world, and notice what happens in my own self during these transitions. I will be speaking about the northern hemisphere, as that is where I live, but do understand that you can align this work with the transitions through southern hemisphere as well, as it is merely the mirror image.

Each solstice or equinox, I create a celebration to connect to the specific energy that is definitive of the particular time of year. I am going to speak about community later in this book, but I do want you to consider that these celebrations are great times to share with others as you create a shamanic community. For now, I will share with you what I do when I am celebrating these special times without others in attendance. Certainly, when I began this work, I was generally doing rituals on my own, or at best with my loving husband. The solstices and equinoxes mark very important shifts in our yearly cycle, and I feel acknowledging and participating in them by honoring them in the best way that I can is paramount in my reconnection to self and the energy of the natural world.

The equinox on or around March 21st marks the beginning of spring in my part of the world. Although this date is an equinox, meaning that the light and dark are supposedly equal in length, because I live relatively far north, the days are still a bit shorter than the nights. This period is when we are definitely seeing an increase in light, however, as the days are getting longer. Things are coming to life, after a dark winter. Where I live, the days are lengthening, and the sun is rising about 7:30am and setting at about 6pm. I personally feel that I am beginning to awaken from the reflective, introspective wintertime, and I start to feel excitement about the new season of growth. This time is not quite the appropriate time in my area to begin gardening or farming, but plans are being made for the growing season ahead. We are reaching a point of balancing the light and dark.

I mark this exciting new period of potential growth with a ritual of intention setting. I set intentions for nurturing a specific attribute that I am ready to work on for myself, that brings me into more harmony or balance, for the equinox is indicative of balance. It is the balancing of light and dark, day and night, and there is an opportunity for looking inward to exploring what may be requiring balance within me. For example, I may set the intention to nurture my creativity in a loving way, as I have not felt balanced in that area of my life. I may set an intention to be open to meeting new people or deepening a relationship, as I may have been isolated over the winter. I do not attempt to limit myself when I set intentions and, for this powerful time of growth potential, I often have a list of personal challenges for growth that I wish to work on as the light increases around me. Metaphorically, as the light is increasing in the day, I set intentions to allow myself to increase my own light, in a balanced and healthy way. This distills into healing the more "shadowy" aspects of myself, either by directly challenging these aspects as I gain awareness of them, or conversely by nurturing my own beautiful, loving light-filled aspects. The increasing light of the season assists me, by shining light on the loving parts of me, and also allows me to focus on the qualities that I wish to change or nurture. I am sensitive to the balancing energetic aspect of this equinox, with respect to equality, harmony, and challenging versus nurturing, and to having a balanced perspective to the best of my abilities.

I prepare a space in my home for the ceremony. March is often an unpredictable time with the weather where I live, so, although it is always great to be out of doors to be in ritual or celebration, I always have a contingency plan for an indoor celebration. As you may be living in a place that does not allow you to be out of doors, I offer the following suggestions for an indoor ceremony. The events do not need to be flamboyant or lengthy, but I feel that by gifting yourself the time to be in a state of compassion and love, you support your growth and connectedness to Spirit. This builds on your daily rituals and begins to open more doors to the vast world of inspiration and oneness.

In your special area, i.e. at your altar or your place of sanctuary, or even in your living room for this particular once-per-year ritual, prepare your items: have a candle to be lit for the ceremony, your rattle, drum, or CD of these sacred instruments, or a CD of beautiful, transformative music. For this particular ceremony, I like to make an offering of lovely spices, sweets and sacred herbs for the helping spirits, so have these on hand. I make little packages containing sage, sweet grass, rose petals, lavender, sandalwood, Palo Santos, patchouli, cedar, cinnamon sticks, dried orange peel and the like. I get all these ingredients at a local health food store, and I do like to have delightful, fresh items to use in ceremony. I make small packages with these items, using the paper containing my written intentions as wrappers. You will also need something in which to burn these items. For indoor ceremonies, I have a fairly large brass bowl, or a beautiful blown glass ashtray that I rescued in a garage sale for this purpose. There are also larger abalone shells available at most metaphysical stores, if you look in the area where the smudging tools are. Please be sure to keep your own safety and that of your neighbors in mind. Be wary if you have a very sensitive smoke detector, and if so, there are some smokeless ways to release your intentions and gifts to the spirits. You might use essential oil sprays of the sacred grasses and plants, which are readily available, and offer your intentions and gifts to the spirits in a beautiful smelling picture, or a perfumed love letter that remains on your altar for the next quarter. There are always creative ways to achieve the same results through blessings, prayers, meditations and journeys performed with reverence and love.

I would also encourage you to explore placing your intentions in all of the sacred elements. With the theme of *balance* being so prevalent at this time of equal light and dark, what would represent balance and harmony for you? Burning your intentions in a smudge bowl represents the element of fire. Perhaps you could release your intentions into water, by placing a glass of clear water over a paper on which you have written intentions, and leaving it there overnight. The essential energy, and the power of your intentions becomes infused in the water. It is an amazing conduit of energy! Once infused in the water overnight, you could drink the water, visualizing your intention merging and strengthening into your own personal vibrant energy.

Consider the element of earth, whereby you might be moved to bury your list of intentions like seeds in a garden. Maybe using a window box or placing them in a bowl of decorative sand that will remain on your altar would feel appropriate?

And what about the element of air? Consider blowing your intentions, one by one into the petals of a rose, and letting these rose petals dry on your altar, or place them lovingly in a beautiful bowl. Ask your guides and teachers what would be the most appropriate method or combination of methods that would be best for you. You might be very surprised that they will offer a new and unique suggestion that is even more resonant to you.

Open space for your celebration, using the method in Chapter Ten, or your own version of invocation. Acknowledge this sacred time of year. It is a time of new beginnings and you have set an intention to honor this time by planting the seeds of intentions of personal and spiritual growth to be achieved in a balanced way. You can then sit down to prepare your intentions in writing, and create the appropriate vehicle for releasing them into the Universe for Spirit to support them (via fire, air, water or earth, as mentioned above, or by your own spiritually inspired method). The ceremony lasts as long as it takes to write all your intentions, wrap them, or blow them into the petals, or other loving container, with love and reverence.

Close the ceremonial space by thanking all your helping spirits, and also by thanking yourself for having the courage to invoke these intentions. Thank the spirits for the abundance, love, presence, groundedness, balance, connection, and courage that you have in your life, and for all that you are prepared to integrate into your life. Feel what is happening in your physical body. Take a few cleansing breaths as you bring your energy fully back into your body and the present moment.

The summer solstice, around June 21st, is a festival honoring light. This is the longest day, the most light-filled day of the year. It is certainly a cause for celebration!

In the work that I do, I see the importance of light energy and how it feeds us, heals us, and represents our own vibrant energy. Increasing our light raises our energy in every way. I believe strongly that we are beings of light energy, and that as we heal and remember our wholeness, our own energetic light gets brighter and brighter. I also believe that as we recognize and become our most radiant light, we affect healing and wholeness throughout the world, including the planet on which we live.

For this healing work, I feel the sun is a powerful metaphor. The sun is always shining, even if there is a layer of cloud hiding the solar disc from our vision. The sun is the light that allows everything to grow, and in this capacity, asks for nothing in return. This is true compassion, and a beautiful example of loving without attachment to an outcome. The sun just shines, and we can learn a lot from that. The sun doesn't choose not to shine because it's having a bad day. He is up there shining with the most radiant light, no matter what. Think what our world would be like if we shone our light in this powerful and loving way, without any attachment or expectation.

To celebrate this season of light, I create a ceremony that is filled with light. Although this is an incredible time to celebrate outside in the warmth of the sun, I do understand that you are probably reading this particular book to offer ideas about what to do within your urban environment, so I will again offer a celebration that can be performed indoors.

I personally like to honor this day in the morning and evening, as it is light where I live from about 3am to 11pm at this time of year. When I arise in the morning, I sing to the morning sun. I thank him for being in my life so selflessly, and I smudge myself on this most light-filled day. My intention is to allow myself to be as bright a light as I can be and shine with love throughout the day. The smudge releases from me anything that keeps me separate from being my most luminous light.

For the evening, I will decorate my sacred space with light. I have extra candles (remember to be safe!) and I will hang little white indoor Christmas lights in the sacred space that I am using for the ceremony. In this celebration of light, I like to offer beautiful and fragrant flower petals to the Spirits in the form of rose petals. I love the fragrance of them, and I know that the Spirits do, too. This is a celebration of light, so the offerings are generally white or yellow petals, which will go into my smudge bowl, along with sage, cedar or sweet grass, or I place vases of beautiful white flowers around my room as an offering. For the releasing portion of the celebration, which I will explain in more detail shortly, I use red petals, and you will need a shell, bowl or vessel to contain them. For this purpose, when it is a personal ceremony, with just myself present, two or three red roses will probably be sufficient, although, I will buy more if I am guided to.

The intention for this ceremony is to offer your light to the Universe in a selfless way, by asking to release from yourself, anything that keeps you from being your most radiant light.

Begin with the opening of sacred space, as directed earlier. Remember to clearly state your intention, and you may always add or change any part of the intention and/or the invocation that makes it more personal or resonant for you. I do like to use some of the white or yellow rose petals in my smudge, as they smell lovely, and they evoke an opening of the heart space.

Once you have created the space, remember your intention: you are intending to be open to releasing whatever keeps you separate from being your most radiant light. Feel what is happening in your body as your spirit guides assist you. They may show you what you can release, or you will sense or hear or feel what is holding you back, so to speak. For this ceremony, when you feel the tangible energy, or the emotion that is keeping you separate, I suggest you will know it. You will feel it rise up in your body as a thickness, or a painful or blocking sensation. You may "hear" a word or phrase that defines this energy. You may not need to know what this blockage is, or what the story surrounding it is. You do not need to know or define or label this blockage... it is just time to let it go. Take a petal or two from your red rose and blow this energy into the rose, thanking the energy for being ready to be released. Place the red petals in a shell or vessel of some type. These petals are going to be released back into the Universe.

Please do not be fearful or judgmental of blocked energy. There is no *bad* energy. This is just energy, and it will be recycled by the Universe without any bias. There is only energy in the Universe, nothing is judged as being good or bad. You may have received some idea around what you are required to release, but don't worry if you don't. Blow this unnecessary energy from the bottom of your abdomen into these petals, and pluck more petals to blow into, until you feel, sense, or know this energy has been lifted from you.

Feel yourself begin to radiate a brighter light with each out breath of release. Remind the Spirits of your intention: you are releasing what no longer serves you. You are releasing what keeps you from shining your most radiant light. Keep scanning your body, and blowing the unneeded energy into the red petals, and placing these petals into the receptacle that you are using for recycling. Notice how you are feeling. Note, without judgment, where you feel yourself becoming more and more light filled. Notice where you feel you are not as filled with light. Blow out the energy from these places that feel less light filled. Your out breath is powerful, and as you release what no longer serves you at this time, it creates a space. This space will be filled with light on your next inhale!

As you become lighter, and brighter, allow yourself to be shown by your guides what it feels like to shine like the sun. How does it feel to shine without any attachment to an outcome?

How does it feel to be a star in the night sky, shining beautifully all the time? You do not need to beam your light anywhere in particular, just shine, and know that this is a moment of complete presence and perfection in your wholeness.

This state of being in radiance and transmutation of energy is called "transfiguration" by Sandra Ingerman, and is described in her book, *Medicine for the Earth*. I recommend reading this wonderful book, as an inspiration for healing ourselves and our planet. In the state of *enlightenment* we are powerful beings of divine and spiritual light, affecting healing all around us, without directing it. We are fulfilling our truth of existence in this state of radiance.

Allow yourself to be in this state for as long as you want. Sometimes, it is helpful to chant or tone to maintain a state of transfiguration. I love being in this state of lightness, and my intention is to do my best in being in this state as much as possible.

Thank your guides and teachers for supporting you thus far, and now, it is time for releasing the red petals holding your unneeded energy back into the Universe. You can burn the petals in the shell that you have put them into, if you wish, and if it is safe to do so. You might signify the total release of the energy by scattering them on water, should you have a pond or river near you. You can release them to Mother Earth, by burying them, with love and gratitude. You might scatter them outside on your walk to work, thanking them as you walk. I also like to put them in a pot of water on the stove and visualize the steam and bubbles completing this ritual, releasing the energy into the Universe. You can dispose of the rose water easily down the sink after that. You might leave the bowl of petals on your balcony outside, in the sun, to allow the further release into the Universe. Energetically, since you are *releasing* through this ritual, don't bath or spray the rose water on yourself, or use the rose petals in your bathwater. This would infer taking the energy back in to your being. Complete your releasing this energy by tangibly letting it go.

September 21st, or thereabouts, is the fall equinox, again where the day and night are almost equal in length. This is traditionally a time for giving thanks. Historically, we gave thanks for the harvest, gratitude for the summer, and preparations were then made for the winter months ahead. My adopted Stoney brother also says that as the leaves drop from the trees, the spirits of those who have passed that year are free to travel home. To go home is always cause for celebration.

For me, the fall is my favorite time of year! It is the New Year for me, a time of transition of the old and preparation for the next phase, and I find it very exciting. This powerful time of year is acknowledging balancing. We can balance the openness to all possibilities with trusting that it is safe to allow this opening. We can allow growth, and balance that growth with the integration of the wisdom that has been received. This transitional season offers balance in the releasing of fear, and the nurturing of trust. It offers the releasing of resistance, and opening to growth, as well as releasing with gratitude the ignorance of our externally focused mind, and sincerely beginning to walk the walk of integrating what we are bringing into our hearts into our daily life.

The celebration of this equinox is in the transitional nature of the season. As the leaves fall, it offers space for movement and integration. As the frost comes, sending many of the plants back to a dormant state, we are offered an opportunity to show our gratitude of the abundance we have received.

As you have been getting to know yourself in such a deep way with all of the inner work that you are doing, I am sure that you are recognizing the many things that you are grateful for. The gifts of presence and self-love, and the connections and relationships that you are establishing and deepening with your spirit guides will no doubt be creating changes within you. The awareness of these changes and the awareness of your emotions and feelings in your body are priceless gifts, for which you can be very grateful. You should have immense gratitude to your Guides and also to yourself for having the courage and commitment to explore your inner world.

It is this sense of gratitude, thankfulness and the blessings that we receive throughout our life that I celebrate at this equinox. It is an acknowledgement of courage and strength of commitment that supports this thankfulness.

For this celebration, I use decorations that represent the colors of the fall. We have many beautiful flowers of bright shades of yellow, orange, purples and reds. I love to decorate my sacred space with beautiful reminders of the harvest. I generally harvest my own sweet grass and sage, and that will dry on a shelf in our kitchen. I use these sacred grasses and herbs all year in my rituals and ceremonies. These smudge tools are always available at metaphysical stores, and often, if the storeowner has any connection to the local First Nations folk, he will have some that has recently been harvested. These fragrant plants make the house smell great! I also try to find lavender plants that have been harvested whole, and dried. I love to have their fragrant essence in vases around my house. I use the dried lavender in my smudge now that I have this year's harvested plants available. It smells fantastic as it burns and I find the affects of the smell of this gorgeous herb so soothing, relaxing and healing.

In your sacred space, have at hand your candle, smudge, with lavender if you choose, on your altar, which will also represent the elements, and the precious things that you hold dear. As an offering to the helping spirits, I would suggest dried flowers, lavender, sage or sweet grass to be burned, representing the element of fire. Perhaps your offering could be through the element of water, with a beautiful bottle of scented water to remain on the altar for a while. Earth, represented by burying or scattering the offering on the ground, may be the element of choice. Perhaps you resonate with air, with an offering blown with your breath into the air or into a flower petal.

Then, find a small rock. This rock should be at least smaller than your hand, and even smaller if you choose. It is going to become part of your altar during this celebration, so choose a rock that you really like, or let it choose you. You might be moved to buy a crystal or semi-precious gem from you favorite metaphysical store, or you may see a stone on your daily walk that speaks to you.

The intention for this celebration is, with your deepest gratitude, to thank all the helping spirits for supporting you throughout the year. Acknowledge that you are grateful for the courage, commitment, and strength that you have acted on, that has facilitated and supported your journey to this point. Recognize and appreciate the depths of understanding and trust that you have reached at this time. Intend to continue this self-exploration with love, compassion, awareness, fearlessness and presence. Ask for guidance as to what quality or strength you can nurture over the winter that will best serve your ongoing spiritual growth and healing.

As always, open space in the way similar to that which I have suggested, adding in your own words, or personalizing the invocation in whatever way feels right to you. Smudge yourself with the sage and, if appropriate to you, lavender. Place your sacred offerings to your helping spirits in whatever way you choose.

Your intention, stated above, is filled with gratitude, and said with commitment, reverence and strength. Ask your helping spirits for the quality or attribute within you that will best serve your spiritual growth now. You will nurture this quality carefully over the winter. Allow the spirits to help you, and listen for their guidance, feeling the sensations in your physical body, and opening to their wisdom.

Perhaps you will hear a word such as courage, or compassion.

Perhaps you will have a sensation in your throat or mouth that might mean that you can nurture loving communication within. Possibly you will just feel the warmth of an energetic hug that feels nurturing, and the aspect of nurturing, or self-love, will be your focus. You will be guided, and you will know what your quality to work with will be. When you have the energy of this important aspect, blow it gently into your rock. You are not letting go of this quality, but you are infusing the rock with this beautiful attribute of your being that you will be nurturing, growing, and reflecting on during the winter. The rock will be your reminder that this quality exists strongly within you, solidly, like a rock, and it grows steadily, easily and beautifully within you in time.

With gratitude, thank your Guidance, and place your reminder rock on your altar with reverence. You may be guided to hold this rock when you are journeying or meditating, or in future celebrations, or you might also be told to put it in your pocket to have it with you during the day.

The days get shorter and the nights longer, as we move toward December 21st, the shortest day. In my northern home, the sunrise happens at about 9am and then sets around 4pm. The sun follows the horizon, low in the sky, during the day. Light seems to be somewhat elusive at this time of year in the northern hemisphere. The long nights are a time of reflection and deep integration for most spiritual walkers, and we relish the time we spend on our inner work in this quieter time.

I understand the challenge of the urban dwellers in this part of the world, and I do understand how dark it can seem sometimes. When I worked corporately, I drove to work and back home in darkness, and was inside a high-rise during the daylight hours. As we approached the darkest day, I noticed the energy of those around me, and I felt how frustrated they were, perhaps without even understanding that it was primarily the lack of light that was causing the moodiness and depression. I, myself, felt very low after many days of not being able to go outside. I did buy a full spectrum light box and used it during my yoga sessions before I left for work in the morning, which was very helpful. Aside from that, though, I vowed to allow all the light energy that I could into my being.

I also looked upon this particular time of year as a time for deep reflection and introspection. This was very helpful, as the gratitude that I had for the time to reflect created a calmness and peace around my day. I was able to let go of some of the frustrations I felt about being "trapped in the dark"! I was reminded that the shaman was the person in the tribe who had this quality about them – they saw in the darkness, and that inspired me to seek Guidance on what would be the most appropriate way to celebrate these times.

During one particularly powerful journey, my spirit guide told me to bring in my own light, and showed me a brightly lit room, filled with beautiful lights. There were candles of all colors, lights all around the room, and in the night sky I could see the Northern Lights. What I understood about this journey was that there were all kinds of light: natural light; sunlight, fire light and the northern lights. There was artificial light with light bulbs of all types. There was reflective light like the moon, or light reflected in a mirror. There were light beings, such as Jesus, Buddha and the like. Then I also knew there was spiritual light, and spiritual lights included the light that I am.

All those types of light inspired me to create a light filled celebration for the darkest day, realizing that the very next day, there would be a tiny bit more light – that light was returning to our hemisphere, just as soon as that very next day. The following day would have a little more light, albeit tiny moments, but moment by moment, light would get brighter. This metaphor was powerful for me as I considered nurturing and brightening my own light.

For this ceremony, you will need lots of lights. I like to use tea lights in the central part of the ceremony, and beautiful Christmas or fairy lights all around the room. We have a room on the north end of our house that has large windows. I love doing this celebration there, as we can see all the beautiful stars out in the sky, and sometimes, when the time is perfect, we are blessed to see Northern Lights. They are so magical! I know that you may not have these beautiful lights available to you for your ceremony, but open up to your creative side, and see what magic you can create in your sacred space. Please remember to be safe if using candles and other open flames. As this solstice is so close to Christmas, perhaps you can include whatever decorations you have up for the holidays. I also love to use holly and boughs of pine around the space, as they are so fragrant and festive. Pine is really flammable, so be very careful.

For the central part of the ritual, I use a large white candle in the center of a round tray. This tray can be of any nonflammable material. I like to use a mirrored tray, as it represents reflected light, which reminds me to be reflective at this important time. You might decorate your tray with rocks, gems, crystals, holly and such. Have the tea lights and a safe lighter handy. You use your smudge, which could be sage or sweet grass, or you might want to try something more appropriate for the season. I buy frankincense tears or chunks of copal or myrrh. These resins are used in parts of the world such as Mexico, Asia and the Middle East and are very exotic when used in ceremonies. As they are resins, they generally require a piece of charcoal burning under them to keep them lit. These charcoal pieces are available at most metaphysical stores.

Light the candle in the center of your tray. Open sacred space as always. The intention for this ceremony is to invite in all types of light to inspire you. This celebration is to express your gratitude for the light being returned at this beautiful time of year, and to offer blessings, thanks and intentions for the new calendar year.

As you face your altar, or the center of the circle in your sacred space, pick up a tea light and set an intention. This intention can be anything that you wish. With reverence, ask for whatever you wish to draw to yourself in the upcoming calendar year. Be creative, humble, loving and compassionate. Maybe you set an intention to recycle. Perhaps you set an intention to do more inner work, perhaps three days a week, instead of one. As you verbalize these intentions, remember there is no judgment. This is not about what you should be doing "better", this is about allowing you to be gentle with yourself: to set yourself free from judgment so that you can grow in all ways.

You can light more candles now and, as you light each one, say another intention. Once you have set all the intentions that feel right or when you feel complete, light gratitude candles. What are you grateful for? Your tray will be getting brighter and brighter. You are increasing the light in your sacred space with all of your intentions and blessings. This is a beautiful representation of the power of your own light, and the brilliance of your being, and the light that is returning to us at this auspicious time.

Notice what you are feeling in your body. Are you resisting, or you going with the flow and having fun? What does the resistance feel like? Can you be open to allowing a little light in? This is such a great celebration of your beauty – can you allow yourself to feel it?

The four ceremonies I have suggested for these powerful times of year can evoke many feelings and emotions and can also indicate to you just how much you are allowing empowerment to develop within you. Do not be self-judgmental, instead, congratulate yourself on your courage, commitment and compassion. These are powerful times of growth and the possibilities for personal healing are incredible!

The calendar holidays are also important, and I do honor these traditional celebrations spiritually – maybe with a bit of a shamanic twist! I feel it is also very important to celebrate and acknowledge all of the special dates like birthdays, rites of passage and weddings. I love to celebrate everything from a house warming to the arrival of a baby. I feel the magic in the special birthdays, like sweet sixteen or ninety. These are all cause for celebration, and a time for considering inviting others to join you on your spiritual journey. I will talk about creating community soon, and will give you some ideas for creating some special celebrations and healing opportunities that you can share with others.

Chapter Twelve

The Elements – or –
Follow the Yellow Brick Road

As I have alluded to several times so far, there are very sacred elements around us. Those of us who live shamanically revere, work with, and honor these elements every day. You have put representations of these sacred items on your altar. We notice the beauty and healing powers of these elements and it is our intention to connect with them in a very deep way, each and every moment. We develop a relationship with each element's healing attributes, and often find that we personally resonate very closely with one particular element.

The elements are: *air, water, fire and earth*. Some cultures even consider *metal* as an element separate from the others. I invite you to explore how that feels for you, and if you would include it in your blessings. For me, there are certain celebrations and certain groups of people that I feel do honor metal specifically as its own element, and I name it in my opening of sacred space, and the invocation. I will speak about this in more detail very soon.

I create rituals and celebrations to honor the elements, and always welcome them into all the healing work and ceremony that I do. When I am working in a certain environment, for example, near a river, I would do a specific ritual to honor water. If I were to be using a particular healing methodology that requires the use of fire for release, I would especially acknowledge the fire.

These are my personal beliefs, but I do find that by strengthening and focusing my gratitude toward the specific healing attributes or transmutation abilities of the element or elements that I am using in a ritual somehow deepens the power and sacredness of that ritual. Anything that opens the participants to being more reverent and in harmony with nature and the elements serves all of us. By honoring the elements, we honor the people that we may be working with as clients, the community, and the planet on which we live.

Air is such a basic requirement. We start our life outside the womb by taking our first breath. The last thing we do on this earth plane is release our last breath. The breath is our source of life, the bridge from our inner world to the outer world. In taking a breath, we breathe in *inspiration*. We literally breathe in *spirit*. I love to sit and breathe consciously in meditation, with this thought of being inspired with every breath in and out.

To honor air, I breathe consciously. I regularly step outside and feel the wind. I visualize, feel, know and sense that the wind is the breath of the spirits. I love to honor air by listening to flute music, which inspires my thoughts and emotional body to reflect on the beauty of the sounds made by air. In Native American traditions, the direction of east is associated with air, and it embodies spiritual awareness. Every moment is marked with a breath and in every moment there is the possibility for a new beginning. With breath, we create sounds with our voice, and we are able to express ourselves.

What represents air on your altar? Is it one beautiful feather, or a bouquet of beautiful feathers? As light as air, the feathers of an airborne being are a beautiful reminder for us to lift any heaviness from our hearts. The ancient Egyptians removed the heart of their pharaohs upon their death, and set the heart on a scale balanced with a feather. If the pharaoh's heart was as light as the feather, it assured them a quick and easy journey to the next land.

If you personally or astrologically resonate with the energy of air – you are high energy, light, containing an air of excitement within you. You are comfortable blowing around easily in the breeze of a day. You might feel at home in the clouds, traveling.

Perhaps your power animal is a bird or another creature that flies.

We all seek enlightenment, and the qualities of air assist us as we consider lifting our luminous bodies to a higher state of being.

Open sacred space in your sanctuary and then practice this beautiful meditation or ceremony for air. Acknowledge the healing qualities of air – which lifts our state of being higher, lifts our wings easily in flight, that we might not be burdened by heaviness of any kind. Drum or rattle or put on a beautiful CD of native flute music to inspire you in feeling the qualities of air in your body. Let air lift from you anything that is no longer required in your being. You may release this on your out breath as you breathe consciously. Imagine the wind blowing through your body, releasing you of what you no longer require. Let air blow away tension, disease, distraction or resistance from you. You simply let the wind take this unneeded energy from you, and let it be recycled! Air transmutes any heavy energy to a neutral state. You may also release any heaviness or dis-ease or resistance from your being by "dancing air". How would you move to embody the qualities of air? With your breath projecting sounds through your voice, how would you sing or vocalize air? This is a very personal celebration, so allow your imagination to be very creative: would you twirl around your room like an autumn leaf? Watch out for the furniture! Or perhaps you would feel more like a gentle summer breeze. Perhaps you remain still, breathing deeply, honoring this life-giving element in silence. Would you allow air to bring forth sounds from within you and vocalize them through song, chanting, or toning? Would you hold a beautiful feather and feel what it must be like to lift up from the surface of the Earth with graceful wings?

Be present with the qualities and meaning of this element and its wonderful lightness until you feel complete. Thank your guides and teachers, and all of the helping spirits for showing you how to honor air.

Fire is a beautiful and very powerful element. It can light our way, heat our homes and keep us warm. Imagine walking up to your house on a dark night, and noticing through the window, that the lights are on, and there is a warm fire burning in the fireplace to greet you. A powerful emotional response of feeling safe, sensing the warmth, and being welcomed is evoked from the warmth of fire. Fire is the element that represents the passion in our heart.

Fire is a powerful way to release unneeded or unwanted energy, and also accepts, carries, and communicates our blessings on the smoke of our smudge. The candle on your altar lights the way for the spirits to find us. As we do our invocation and open space, fire lets the spirits know that we have begun our work. If you resonate with the energy of fire, you may have *very* lively energy. Fire people are often highly demonstrative, passionate, and ramp up to elevated emotional states quite quickly. They frequently move with quick staccato movements, and embody fire's physical energetic aspects. You may be a fire symbol astrologically. If your power animal is a four-legged, or maybe even a dragon, you may have a fire nature. The Native Americans associate fire with the south, a direction most known for bringing change. How do you react or respond to changes in your life? Is this element inspiring you to look at your ability to be flexible in times of change? Do you suddenly feel inspired to clear out the old and prepare for the new?

To honor fire, open your sacred space, as always. Fire is a very moving, highly emotional and passionate element, and may inspire rapid, beautiful dancing. It is a passionate pathway for birthing your desires, and you can now act out these dreams in an ecstatic dance, warming your heart and soul as you move. If you don't feel as energetic, or are not as able to move freely in your space for whatever reason, you can wrap yourself in a warm, cozy blanket and honor the warmth of fire. You might also meditate looking at the flame of your candle, marveling in the beauty and light-filled transformative spiritual nature of this element. The light of the fire shows us the way we need to go to achieve the things we intend and desire. Always end your celebration by showering your guides and teachers with gratitude.

Water is a life-giving element. When we are awaiting our birth to this earthly plane, we are encased in a watery world, safe while we grow and change physically. Our bodies are largely comprised of water, and this is why the moon has such influence over us. Water element people are usually more introspective and are great dreamers. The element of water inspires fluidity and the flow of emotions. This element is female in nature, which means that there is an emotional component to this element. Is your astrological sign a water sign? Water is how we generally cleanse our bodies and our environment. We baptize our children in this holy element. When we look into a pool of water, it reflects our image back to us like a mirror, and inspires growth within us by seeing ourselves in reflection. Water encourages us to "go with the flow", so perhaps the message for you from water may revolve around how you might be resisting, or not allowing, this flow easily in your life. Water hosts power animals who swim, live, hunt or are nurtured by water. In Native American mythology, water energy resides in the west, which is the direction of transitions and death, so that new beginnings can be born. Have something beautiful on your altar to represent water: a bowl or bottle of sacred water, a seashell, or starfish or a picture of a natural body of water that has special meaning to you.

In honoring the healing aspects of water, an intention might revolve around clearing all negative aspects in life, thereby raising vibrational energy. Open sacred space, and place a bowl of water on your altar as you embody your truth and lightness of being. Envision the water in its pure and perfect state. Feel the purity of the water, and its ability to cleanse anything that requires clearing within you. Have a beautiful rose nearby, and blow any of this unnecessary energy into the petals of the rose. Then, with intention, release the petals into the bowl of water. As the petals float, notice that the energy is no longer heavy within you, but floating on the water, cleared from your being, and has been released into its pure and divine state. This is also a beautiful ceremony to perform near open water, such as a lake, river, ocean or stream, as the visualization of the petals drifting away confirms that the energy contained in them is certainly not a part of you anymore.

In your urban space, a bowl of water has the same power to release, as your visualization is held within your thoughts and intentions. I have also heard of some stories of shamanic practitioners who have used a sink or bath full of water for their personal ceremonies for water, and indeed even a couple of people who have used a toilet! Don't ever let your limiting thoughts or preconceived notions of right and wrong stifle your creativity. These ceremonies are for *you* and your helping spirits will guide you to ways of creating the perfect experience that will hold profound meaning for you. If seeing your unneeded or unwanted energy being flushed down the toilet speaks strongly to you, why wouldn't you consider having a beautiful bathroom ceremony for yourself?

You may wish to "dance" water. What would your dance to honor water look like? At the end of your ceremony, be sure to thank your helping spirits for all of their support and love!

Mother Earth is the Mother of All Things. The element, *earth*, may be represented on your altar as a small globe, your favorite crystals, gemstones, or rocks. Perhaps you have a small bowl of sacred ground from a place that you have visited, sand from a wonderful vacation, or a bag of healing salt or minerals. Earth holds the emotional aspects of groundedness, gratitude, nurturing and serenity. If one of your helping spirits is a Standing Person or a tree, your roots might resonate strongly with earth energy. If you are an earth astrological sign, this element may be particularly meaningful for you. Some Native American tribes consider the north as the sacred direction for this element.

After opening sacred space for celebration, honor this element by embracing the energy of the Tree of Life. This tree, which is present in many ancient stories, from all corners of this wonderful planet, is representative of wisdom, observation, being perpetually rooted deeply into the earth. The tree holds ancient wisdom and represents connections to all things: the three worlds: lower; through its roots, middle; in its trunk and branches, and upper with its leaves. It holds the embodiment of ancient stories, which it has observed since the beginning of time, and as we explore a journey through this magnificent tree, we are privy to all of these stories. We are exposed to all manners of healing, all the compassion, love and connection that is possible, as we merge into Oneness.

The Tree of Life shows us how we are all connected through the roots that flow, unseen, in the earth. We all stand uniquely in our trunks, and we touch the sky with our branches. We are limitless as we reach toward the light. In your exploration, how does it feel to *merge* with this tree? How does it feel to touch the center of the earth and reach for the stars in the same moment? The impossible is possible, and there is nothing that can stop this evolution, save your doubts or limiting beliefs. Cast these fears aside and feel the empowerment in being present in the moment, and see all the beauty for miles around through the magnificence of your being! You are in the womb of the earth with your roots, and connected to the Star People with your leaves. What a fantastic sense of infinite possibility!

What would your "earth dance" look like? I'm sure that it would bring in aspects of rootedness, groundedness, nurturing and reverence. If you choose to dance this element, the movements might be slow, deliberate, silent, grounded, like walking purposefully on rice paper. Or perhaps you dance like you are in deep sand. Maybe your dance will represent the trees, flowing and bending in the wind, while rooted in the present moment. Remember when you feel complete with your process, to thank your Guidance and yourself for the compassion and courage to explore.

The elements are a part of all of us. Our bones and the solid parts of our body *is* earth. Our blood is like a great river of water. Our heart holds the fire of our life force. Our breath is the air of our being. Although you may resonate with one or two elements more than others, honor them all in time. Conceivably, you could create a celebration to honor them all at one time, welcoming in the balance of the elements!

The natural world may remind you of an element to honor. For example, connect with the weather. Is it hot and sunny? Would you honor fire at this time? Summer is this element's season. Is the weather wet and rainy? It might require a dance of fire to warm up that dreary day! To honor the spring and the need for rain to germinate seeds, honor water. Maybe the wind is particularly gusty, and you are inspired to celebrate air. If you are feeling lightheaded and ungrounded, for whatever reason, consider a celebration to honor earth to gain groundedness within you.

When you travel, keep the element's healing aspects strong within your being. A trip to the mountains to ski might be well supported by honoring earth the night before your visit there. Who knows what the spirits may offer as a gift when you are skiing the next day?

Remember that even within the context of your urban lifestyle, all the elements are present. We have created a world that looks so different from the one our ancestors lived in. Because you have different stressors, and live in much different surroundings, consider how you can bring the elements into your life *today*. If you only focus on what doesn't seem natural in your world, you might be resisting some of the possibilities that are available to you now. As I mentioned earlier, you are creating your reality. How about working *with* what is currently available in a compassionate and loving way, so that you can shift, change and grow, and create beauty in your life, no matter what? You can create peace and tranquility no matter what is going on around you. Remember that the disconnection from the natural world is a major cause of disease and illness in our modern world.

For several years, I have led a meditation class in an office building in a nearby city. As I mentioned, I live rurally, where it is very quiet, and perhaps the loudest noise I ever hear is a winter north wind, or, now and again, an airplane. I really noticed that when I began leading the class through a guided meditation or journey, I was noticing all the sounds of the traffic outside. The office that I am blessed to use for this class is at the corner of two of the busiest roads in the city, with the Trans Canada Highway running below, right outside of the window!

Huge semi-trailer trucks, loudly starting to move from the lights, shifting gears as they accelerated, punctuated my words as I attempted to guide the participants into stillness. Inside of me, as a beginner teacher at the time was the fear that I couldn't possibly assist these people in their practice. What I came to realize was that the noise supported my own learning, and that I could shift my own perspective to let go of the resistance that I was creating, because it brought up such great fear of failure in me. I was worried about the participant's experience in that they would not enjoy themselves! I was trying to please them, and make them feel better so that I would feel better. That was very fear-based behavior on my part, and when I asked for guidance on how to *fix* the situation, my guides started to laugh. They reminded me that the situation was perfect for my learning. They showed me a picture of a small child in the holocaust, gently playing a violin as the bombs went off around him. I knew what they meant: peace can only be found within.

When I focused my attention on the perfection and divine wisdom being shared by Guidance in the moment, the noise went away. I was able to be in the middle of the perfect storm, in tranquility, and share that with my students by guiding them with compassion into their own personal experience.

With this in mind, your environment is perfect for you, just as it was in that classroom for me. I was required to learn about all the possibilities of connecting with my Spirit Helpers instead of resisting the power of the stillness, by focusing on the external chaos. By shifting my perspective even slightly, the noise, which really was within me, created by me to learn about myself, was quelled by opening to the quiet. I was able to see the environment in its completeness; its perfection, and open myself to the expansiveness of connecting with all things, even on that busy intersection.

For these modern times, *metal* is one of the elements that I believe we need to work with, merge with, and consider what it offers. The metal in the vehicles outside the meditation room that I perceived as so noisy and disruptive is of service to us all. If I can see the perfection of the vehicles' being in this moment, I begin to work *with* them in trust, not *against* them in fear and frustration. When I allow myself to see, sense, feel and know how this is all part of my experience, and not to resist what perfection lies beneath the apparently noisy surface, I can receive insights, guidance and wisdom.

On the surface, merging with, or understanding deeply the essence of *metal* might seem difficult, but think about metal in its various states. It is a liquid when heated to very high temperatures. It is a solid at most moderate temperatures. It expands and contracts with temperature changes. It is flexible, too, if you have watched a bridge or a large structure closely; it actually moves. Have you worn a ring or bracelet that has changed shape when you caught it on something or leaned hard against it? In perhaps very subtle ways, metal teaches us to be flexible, shifting and transforming and adapting to changing circumstances with grace and ease.

Through neglect, misuse or overuse, some metals rust. How can we nurture and best use this element without it falling into misuse or neglect?

How do we honor this amazing element that is so universally present in our lives?

As always, create sacred space, invoking the support of all the helping spirits. Set an intention to merge with the essence of metal, and learn from its qualities and aspects. I immediately think of the stories of the ancient alchemists who were supposedly changing lead into gold. As I know that many stories of old were of a metaphoric nature, and have gone through thousands of years of translation and passing down, I extract what this particular story means for me. An alchemist, who was perhaps even a shaman, was shifting something darker and more unrefined into something that is beautiful, shimmering in the light, and of a higher value and quality. This is the infamous story of turning lead into gold; a metaphorical message of our spirit becoming lighter, or becoming enlightened through trans-formation and transmutation of energy.

I feel what I am feeling in my body, which I acknowledge is a sense of expansion and knowing. My sense is that the deeper meaning of this tale is more about shifting energy from dark to light, and specifically may be a reflection of how we as humans grow and shift as we become *enlightened*. What if the message is to be an alchemist, and by doing our best inner work, with intention and love, transmute our own energy from within from a state of fear, which may be construed as somewhat lead like, to a state of love, which is radiant and luminous, like gold? This analogy becomes a story of spiritual growth, of enlightenment! This is the inspiration for my tribute to and celebration of the element of metal.

For this ceremony, gather metal objects that represent the

shapeshifting qualities of metal, and of its luminosity, once transmuted to the purest forms. I might decorate my sacred space with glitter and shiny metal candleholders. I use a brass bowl for my smudge. I consider items that change when heated or cooled. For the smudge, I might use resin, heated with a charcoal disc, rather than my usual sage, or burn a combination of these sacred items. I embrace the ideas of transmutation of energy, and am open to all the things that the helping spirits might offer. I might wear jewelry made of metal, or gemstones that have a luminous quality to them. During this particular ceremony, I might play a brass Tibetan singing bowl, to allow the metal to express its beautiful sound. I employ bells made of various metals to accompany the sounds of the bowls.

When I look at and examine the transformational qualities of metal, and its ability to take form in different states, I might be inspired to move. What would your dance for metal look like? Might you sway to the music of the Tibetan bowls, or dance lightly with the bells. Wrap your heart around the transformational and flexible element of metal. Feel your gratitude for the gifts this element offers. How many wonderful things we have in our lives to use because of this element: tools, shelter, vehicles, medical equipment, and vessels for cooking in. Metal is widely used in our world.

When you feel complete with your expression of gratitude for this precious element, be sure to thank your Guidance and helping spirits. Don't forget to have gratitude for your own participation in this experiment of insight, and indeed for your participation in Life.

Your awareness and presence is key in integrating the elements into your practice of inner exploration. Keep practicing, as you support yourself in growing with a strength created in balance with all elemental aspects. As you allow the elements to resonate within you, you connect to your outer world in a much different and more integrative way.

Chapter Thirteen

The Community – or –
Taking Public Transportation?

If you are practicing your inner work with love and compassion you are probably beginning to notice that you are connecting with others *differently*. Perhaps you feel like you want to get to know your colleagues in a deeper capacity, or that you are more interested about their lives. Are you noticing that they are more interested in what you are doing? I feel that as we move into a more introspective and conscious existence personally, we begin to attract different people into our lives. We might find that we are more curious about our fellow students in the Earth School, mostly because we are living with more curiosity and excitement about our own lives.

We begin to experience more illuminating interactions with the faces that we have seen in the lineup at the coffee shop. We are moved to speak with the clerk at the bank, and are genuinely interested in their response, whereas we were polite and superficial previously. When we open up our lives with awareness and allowing, this openness allows others in, too.

This might be a challenge for you, or you might welcome this with open arms. Sometimes, I have felt quite overwhelmed when I realized that living my life on the shamanic path seemed to be drawing in people who wanted to know more about me, and learn about my spiritual practice. Perhaps they felt a certain peacefulness around me that wasn't there before, and this caused them to be curious. I do feel that when people feel a shift in energy in someone else, that on some level, even if it is not conscious, they know or feel it. People began asking me for my opinion on a lot of subjects, and told me that they knew that my answer would have a different perspective than other people they might have asked.

When I left my corporate job, and opened my healing practice full time, fears within me were triggered around facing people, in the capacity of counseling them or assisting them on their spiritual path. I was not used to having many people come to my home, and sometimes I would feel that people were trying to "invade" my privacy! I had been doing a lot of inner work for myself, and knew that the pain that I was feeling within my body was telling me that I was reacting to this so called invasion from fear. During my life, when these fears were very active in me, my reaction was to withdraw. Now, by having the full support of the Universe behind me, as always, I was being supported in facing a possibility of choice in this new situation. Was I going to melt into the wallpaper, or challenge my deepest fears and step into the light, where I could share my gifts by assisting others in their healing, as, co-incidentally, I was healing myself?

Often with strong and persistent resistance present and active within me, I did manage to challenge my fear. Rather than retire into a hermit-like life, which is what Fear wanted me to do, I took steps to increase my confidence, nurture my healthy qualities, and interact with others in a very deep way. Despite feeling afraid, inadequate or unworthy, I kept on scheduling client appointments. I noticed the sensations in my body when the car of a client drove up the driveway and I secretly wished they would turn around and leave. I invited them in and supported them in spite of the shy hermit within me that was worried that they would be disappointed in me.

I knew that each client that came to me was a source of healing for me. I realized that as I was doing my own inner work, and setting an intention to heal, that I developed a deeper empathy and understanding for my clients. All healers need to be on their own healing path.

Each and every client that I saw, and still see, reminds me of things that I can heal more deeply within myself, and that everything that I say to a client, in support of their healing, is something that I need to hear for myself. I am convinced that all the words and thoughts that I share with my clients during our sessions do not come from me, but are the perfect healing message that Guidance is verbalizing through me for the client and myself.

So I recognize, and I hope you recognize too, that interaction and relationship with others is the next natural step in our evolution. We cannot grow to our spiritual potential in isolation. I know this because I tried it, and it doesn't work.

In a journey with my spirit guide who helps me challenge my own inner fears in personal transformation, I asked how I could affect my healing more deeply, and let go of the deep-seated resistance that was distracting me and keeping me separate from being the empowered healer that, deep down, I felt I could be. I was shown a vision of myself in a large circle of people, leading a ceremony. My entire being was radiant and glowing, and so were all the others in the circle. Well, despite any of my complaints, excuses or reluctance to creating an event, I knew I was going to have to at least try! What I lacked in confidence and enthusiasm, I made up for with my stubbornness and bull headedness. Or perhaps, I knew that my Guidance was correct, and I actually need to stop arguing with them.

My first community event was a potluck dinner held at the winter solstice. I had invited a few friends, telling myself the "story" that the 21st of December was close enough to Christmas that I could cover up for any of my fears of being thought of as weird or "out there" by saying it was "just" a Christmas gathering. Just in case anything went "wrong", I was fairly careful when creating the guest list. There was really no one I felt particularly threatened by, or who wouldn't speak to me again should they get too weirded out by the activities I was planning! I had invited a couple of people that I worked with, as this was before I left the corporate world, and a fellow that my husband worked with was coming with his wife. My sister came, as did a couple of lifelong friends. My daughter and a couple of her friends were there, too.

I must admit, I initially over-thought the evening, planning every detail, and yes, I did realize that I had attachment to the outcome! Although I was becoming increasingly nervous, I challenged those fears by releasing my attachment to my extensive "to do" list right after we had finished eating. The complicated and detailed ceremony that I had planned and scripted was set aside. I took a few deep, clearing breaths. I shared with my guests that I wanted to experiment with a small ceremony to acknowledge this potent time of year, and I wondered if they would like to join me. Well, surprisingly, in a few short moments, we were all standing in a circle in my meditation room. The room was lit up with candles and soft light was emanating from a salt lamp and an amethyst lamp.

I welcomed everyone there. I smudged the group, telling them briefly the purpose of smudging. Once that was completed, I shared my intention for our circle together. I hoped that they would be willing to speak about what they were grateful for at this time of year, whose theme was so filled with the joys of giving and receiving. I had a large skein of red wool in my hand. After I shared what I was grateful for, I held onto the end of the wool, and tossed the skein across the circle. The recipient of the skein then shared their gratitude and, as she held onto the wool that was connected to me, tossed the skein to another person across from her in the circle. This continued on until everyone had shared. We all looked at the beautiful web of wool connecting us all. We talked about how this was a visible reminder of our connection as human beings who had the potential to make a difference in the world. It was a simple, but beautiful way to share something wonderful at the Christmas season!

Everyone who was there said they had had a good time, and

wanted to know when I was going to do something like that again. I smile to myself as I share this story now, as I do remember it being quite traumatic for me at that time. Now, I honestly don't worry or stress about creating these events at all.

Humans in the evolving consciousness are thirsting for community, and that little celebration took on much more meaning for those present. I know that there were some emotions triggered, but the experience was perfectly appropriate for that person. I did my best to create a safe place for people to share, and I believe that the environment was supportive to them, no matter what was going on inside for each individual.

Some people shared that they felt warm and comfortable. One friend felt a bit embarrassed about her failed toss of the skein of wool, but not only did everyone allow her a second, and then a third attempt to toss the skein right across the circle, but everyone was smiling and having fun, supporting her as she threw the wool. I'm sure that some of the people were worried about their toss, and perhaps they were happy that her experience wasn't theirs, but what a wonderful way to help each other with humor and lightness while creating a sense of togetherness!

I stopped worrying about whether everyone was enjoying themselves and was present in my own body, having my own insights and experiences, which was a wonderful opportunity for learning and healing for me.

We also heard what all our friends were grateful for. What a lovely way to know your companions better, and connect with them in a heartfelt way. Not one person wanted to leave early, and after the ceremony, the laughter and conversation was a fabulous reflection of the deepening of friendships and newfound comfort we felt with each other.

That was the beginning of my creating events to include others. In spite of myself and my fears and my worries, I had begun to create a community. Having others join me in my celebrations of life allowed me to face my fears, and develop strength in myself that I don't believe would have happened otherwise. I have since been inspired to take courses in teaching and assisting others to enrich their own lives, and I have even overcome my fear of writing some of these experiences down in this book to share with you.

Recently, I officiated at a beautiful wedding for two very special friends, and that was a magical experience. I believe that when we face our fears head on, with an intention to heal, we nurture ourselves deeply, and we are reminded of our wholeness. We are not broken. We have just forgotten what it is like to be Light! We forget how wonderful and precious we are in the Universe, and how well the Universe supports us each and every day to be and do our best.

What are you noticing in your circle of friends as you continue this inner work? Do you see a shift or change in this circle? Are the relationships that you have had for a while changing? Are you courageous in saying what you need or want to share about the experiences that you are having as you delve into the deeper aspects of yourself?

Sometimes these shifts are subtle, and we only notice them upon reflection. For instance, in my corner office, decorated with a lovely salt lamp, with soft music playing on the radio or on a CD, I noticed that more and more colleagues would come into my office to chat. One person even said that they loved to come and visit my office because something about it made them feel relaxed. I might have taken that opportunity to tell them how I felt really relaxed that day, or that I had had a particularly great meditation that morning, or that I did thirty minutes of yoga rather than twenty when I woke up that day.

Perhaps I had gone for a beautiful walk at lunchtime, and I could invite them to go with me the next day. My intention for sharing those things would be to create connection with this person, not to brag about my "spirituality" or make them feel like they were less than me. These are all compassionate inroads for creating a deeper connection. I was supporting my own wellness in my office space, and it drew in people who resonated with creating wellness within them. People were always saying that they would rather meet in my office than anyone else's, which was very telling, I thought.

Although we might have been discussing something regarding work, we could get off on a tangent as I sensed that they wanted to remain in the space as long as they could. At some level, they really did feel something different inside of themselves when they were in my office, sharing. If they were open, I might tell them that I regularly smudged my office. I might open a discussion about what they felt when they were in their own office. It was really interesting what might come up as they thought about that.

My husband, Mike, runs heavy equipment, and is constantly around construction workers, usually men. I know that when he began his own inner work, it was difficult for him to share that part of his life with anyone there. It created fear within him of not being accepted or being ridiculed by the guys. He has always exhibited courage, however, and would sometimes respond in a tense situation with sharing what he was feeling.

Sometimes the responses from his colleagues were fairly subtle, or at the very least pretty humorous. His co-workers began to talk about him as the "guy who is always talking about that 'feeling' stuff", or that "guy who is always looking for the positive #$#% in everything!" I thought that it was wonderful to be perceived in this way.

What I find really interesting is that one or two of these fellows have actually had quite deep and insightful conversations with my husband! One fellow spoke with Mike because he sensed that there were ghosts in his house. After speaking at length about this, this so-called "rough" or "tough" construction worker engaged me to clear the house of this energy. We had a circle of about a dozen people at this session, including another of Mike's colleagues from work. There was openness where we had least expected it.

We talked about what we felt in the house, and what the experiences were of the people who lived there. I went around the house, clearing with sage and speaking to the entities that continued to live there. There were several. Not once did anyone laugh, and nobody left the ceremony. Some profound intuition came up for me regarding one man living in the house, and it turned out that his mother-in-law had recently passed. The images I saw were of a very personal item that he cherished, that had belonged to this special woman. He was deeply moved that this particular item, which was an important way of remembering his mother-in-law, had come to light out of the reading. It was a wonderful evening full of sharing and there was a palpable change of energy to one of lightness once the misplaced energy was released.

Since that particular event, the same co-workers and others from Mike's crew have attended our celebrations and events. One even turned up at a couple of yoga classes! I think this is fabulous. As I said earlier, we are all seeking others to share with. We are all seeking our tribes.

I have set an intention to be aware when others are reaching out to me to support their healing, or to create community. I have a friend I have known for many years now, and we have always been able to speak about things that were probably not considered your typical mainstream conversations. This beautiful friend was an ICU nurse when I met her when our young children began riding lessons.

I felt like I had known this woman forever, and I never felt like I had to guard anything that I said to her. We talked about *everything*. I learned that she had a very strong spiritual side to her, and was also, through her work in the hospital, very insightful and curious about the experiences patients had when they had near-death experiences. She was present with many patients when they were transitioning. My friend had experienced many paranormal events, including a very significant series of omens after her father had passed.

Not long after I met her, and became instant friends, my own mother became gravely ill and my beautiful new friend was an angel sent to us from the Universe to support me during my mother's transition. This wonderful friend worked in the ICU where my mom spent her final days on Earth.

My friend and I have gone through many of life's lessons together, most recently the passing of her own mother, and our friendship has continued to deepen and flourish as we support each other through these sometimes difficult lessons.

When this same friend said to me not too long ago over a coffee that she knew of someone that she felt would be a really good connection for me for networking for my healing practice, I felt a strong pull of energy around my heart. I just knew she was right, and there was something special that was being created. After being introduced, this new friend and I went for coffee or on long walks, where we shared deeply personal insights in support of one another. We have co-created events together, and we are expanding our circles widely to share the important work that we are doing. She has encouraged me to stretch myself and to think outside of the box to create bigger and more challenging teaching opportunities, all the while, learning so much about myself. Recently, we held an event for women, which was a beautiful healing space for all who attended.

It is so amazing to me how supported we all are by the Universe and our loving guides and teachers, when we really listen and act on the opportunities with our most loving intentions and self-compassion. Our Earth-bound helpers are all around us!

The opportunities to dream a different dream collectively are expanded exponentially when we work together in community.

There are many books and studies regarding the quantum properties of energy, and how this relates to prayer, positive thinking, intentions and healing. Having two people work together is not twice the power of one working alone, but is exponentially more powerful.

I have heard highly educated mathematicians and quantum physicists speculate on a formula to calculate how many people it takes to create a positive change in the world. For all the symbols, equations and logic that gets thrown at this problem, my own solution to this esoteric question is – *one*. I honestly believe that if one person makes a positive change for himself or herself, their energy has the potential to shift their entire world. Their vibrational energy has risen, even if it is only slightly.

One person opens to being their most radiant light, and this affects two friends. Those two friends shine their radiant light, and they each affect two friends, and so on and so on. Suddenly, almost instantly, we have many shining their light, and this has affected the collective dream dramatically: the collective dream changes.

In many shamanic journeys that I have taken, and those that have been shared with me by friends, students, and others in my community, the collective vision is that the time to do this new dream work is *now*. In a recent journey that my husband shared with me, his helping spirits told him that the humans were acting like spoiled adolescents. It was time to grow up! In the evolutionary time line, we had gone through our birth, our childhood, and now our awkward teen years. We have treated each other poorly, and treated our Mother, the Earth, badly. It is time to become respectful and act like grown-ups.

Now we are effecting change and healing ourselves, our world, and our planet in awe-inspiring ways, starting with one. You. Me. We have so much awesome potential.

How can we use this potential?

When I look at the headlines, listen to the news on the radio, or even see the television news, I am struck by how much healing is required in the world. I notice the environmental disasters, the economic difficulties, and the violence that people are inflicting on each other. I sense the tragedies and feel the anger and the desperation of the victims of these tragedies. I see the media manipulate the news to maximize the drama or support the opinions of the media moguls. I have heard people talking about conspiracies, and I have just had to take a step back and attempt to observe this from a more objective perspective. If I am able, I take a stance of neutrality, and with awareness, really look at what these circumstances are offering for me to learn about myself.

I admit that there are times when I, too, get caught up in the trauma and the drama of world events. I feel Mother Earth hurting when we have inflicted some terrible disaster on her, like an oil spill. I have precognitive experiences of tsunamis, and yes, I did have some premonitions leading up to 9/11. What I very much need to be aware of, is to not feed the *suffering* with my energy, but to remember to have true compassion. Again, this compassion is not sympathy, but an altruistic sense of envisioning, perceiving and feeling the perfection and light of the circumstance, the people experiencing the disaster, and the planet herself. Remember we are all energy and light. We are all spirits. We are all perfect in our divine light.

Hopefully, and with a clear intention to be in a state of awareness, I can catch myself before I begin to feed more fear into what is going on in the world. To shift the perspective on a disaster, and effect healing on Mother Earth, for instance, I envision her in her perfection. I feel her beauty and sense her healthy heartbeat. I see her clear waters and beautiful forests. I see Mother Earth in her divine light, in a perfect state of health, and my belief is that in holding that *dream*, that visual image of divine light, there is the potential to create that dream into this reality. If I am one person doing that, and creating with as much love and compassion as I am able to, then I feel I have done my very best.

To support others, in my earlier example of a natural disaster, I hold a healing circle. Together, we sit in a loving circle, with a beautiful vision of Mother Earth's state of being as absolutely whole and perfect. We envision the homes and buildings rebuilt and beautiful. We imagine and dream the people healed from their injuries and living well. We do not just imagine these pictures of wholeness and beauty. We embrace and experience it as if it is happening. We feel the air, smell the sweet flowers, and touch the beautiful buildings and the vegetation. We create the dream of wholeness and we then transfigure, holding that dream. I set up an altar in the center of the circle, and I place a globe or another representation of the Earth on this altar. The participants are always invited to place their sacred items on the altar. As in all circles, we open sacred space and smudge, set healing intentions for Mother Earth, and connecting to our Guidance, envision the planet in wholeness.

We are not negating that others have suffered, but we are creating from loving and healing aspects of ourselves. The "sufferers" do not need our sympathy – they require our love and compassion for healing.

Remember the transfiguration process that I offered to you in Chapter Eleven? I feel this is one of the most powerful ways to transmute energy, and with the energy generated in a group, this is a measurable and quantifiable method for healing. Please look at Sandra Ingerman's website and check out the pictures that have been posted regarding the profound changes of energetic states of objects placed in the center of a room while participants transfigured. It is absolutely amazing!

This is the best work that we can be doing to assist the planet. I encourage you to practice this whenever you can, with friends or even by yourself. This is the potential of the *one* that I talked about before. And when the *one* becomes the *ONE*, where there are many joined together energetically in physical presence with each other or holding one healing intention energetically around the world, we can transmute energy powerfully! I have felt the effects of this compassionate work myself.

If you have a few people over at your house, working with healing in Divine Light through transfiguration work, experiment by having half the group sit in the center of the circle, receiving the effects of the outer circle as they radiate light. Remember, the outer circle is not directing energy, just "being" their most radiant light. Have the group share their experiences after the first round of sharing light, and then switch places and share again. My experience in participating in both roles has been wonderful.

You may also wish to experiment with placing bottles or bowls of water on the altar in one of these powerful healing circles. Take a sip of the water before the circle transfigures, and then afterward. The taste is quite different. I believe that this little experiment really offers some estimation of the potential of this work.

As I alluded to earlier in this book, there are groups around the world that join together in a huge virtual circle on each full moon to create what is called a web of light for the purpose of radiating their most divine light. Again, check out Sandra Ingerman's website for more information. I recommend you read about this beautiful monthly occurrence and join in when you can. It is an extremely powerful experience!

When I read about the economic "crisis", I considered the fear-based energy in which it was created. I acknowledged and sent loving compassionate energy to those corporations and banks that were controlling the purse strings, or those people who were grossly over leveraged and were losing their homes, and everyone in between, and didn't judge them. I felt their fear: the greed of some, the desperation of others, and knew that they were creating their own circumstances from a state of fear. I didn't pity them, or sympathize with them in any way. I felt compassion for them, and did my very best to remain in my own wholeness.

There is abundance for all of us. Again, there are life lessons that we have come to the Earth School to experience. Many folks really believe that there is not enough for them. They are creating their reality with a fear of lack. There is not enough for them, and there never will be. Not enough love, not enough money, not enough friends, not enough, not enough. Nor do they feel that they are actually worthy of receiving abundance. That is the reality that they are creating with their fear of unworthiness.

A very interesting journey to do if you feel that you are experiencing creating your life from lack is to journey to the Master of Abundance. See what this powerful entity has to share with you. Where does this Master reside? Is this Master a man or woman? What questions do you have for this wonderful source of information? What do you feel when you are in the presence of this Master or Mistress? Listen carefully to the answers, as they will be given just for you.

What is my part in global healing? First, it is about healing myself, and remembering, as always, my divine light and radiance of being. When I truly believe that there is more than enough loving, healing energy and I am able to receive this love and healing with gratitude and equality, then my perspective is entirely different. I see the lesson expressing itself through me in my circumstances as I am offered choices on how I can move forward.

Will I choose lovingly, or continue on in fear? Sounds easy. I admit, the concept is simple, but putting it into practice isn't always that easy! It takes commitment and courage, just like *all* your inner work. Circumstances and situations sometimes feel overwhelming and difficult. Sometimes, it takes real strength and self-compassion to move through this, remembering that you always have choices available to you, especially when you are embroiled in a very painful experience.

This is when you need to ask for assistance the most. This is when you can call on Guidance to do what they do best. *You* must be prepared to look, listen, and feel.

Pulling yourself out of a highly reactive situation can be challenging, but not impossible. Consider a moment of despair. Can you step back from that moment when the atmosphere is charged with emotion? Can you, even for a moment, take one conscious breath? Once you have begun to shift this energy, even slightly, you can keep breathing consciously. The more space you can create in this highly charged moment, between the activation of fear and the reaction, the more self-empowerment you create with love. Perhaps you can shift your perspective just a little bit. The situation may not stop right away, but you may create a little peace in the moment, so that you can connect with Guidance and find the meaning in this powerful moment.

At these times it is helpful to have a true friend, one who will assist you in recognizing that the circumstances that are triggering you are being provided for you specifically by your co-creative partner, the Universe, to learn something important about yourself. If you have been creating community or sharing your insights of personal growth with anyone else, perhaps you already know someone that you could ask for support. This person is not a friend who will agree with your fears and help you feed them, especially when you are in reaction or suffering. This special person will assist you in looking at the deeper meaning of the situation, and remind you that the Universe is supporting you.

Conversely, perhaps you have realized that you can now be of much more true support to your friends and colleagues. You are creating a wonderful circle of equality and compassion. This is a truly amazing change in the way that we interact in relationship in this emerging consciousness. This is the type of world that I want to be in. That is what the new dream is about.

Chapter Fourteen

Taking Time for You – or – When is the Next Rest Stop?

You have been doing your daily work, journeying all over Non-Ordinary Reality, and having lots of meetings with your spirit guides! Although this work is rewarding and offers a life-changing practice for our growth and healing, we do need to remember that we must provide some time for reflection and integration of the insights being received and empowerment that we are creating for ourselves.

In the Western World, we have so many imbalances in our lives. We are not achieving the work-life balance, despite attending the lectures and workshops that our employers offer for us, telling us how and why we should do just that. We hear all the terms about balancing our family life, work life, and me-time, but very few of us are taking action. We are often working overtime, even taking work home. We take our work to the dinner table, into our family conversations and even into our dreams. We don't get enough sleep and do not leave enough time for balancing work and leisure. We do the same when we embark on our inner work as well.

You may have noticed that after some journeys, you might be a bit reluctant to return to this reality. You might feel a bit disoriented or spaced out. Perhaps you have struggled to fall asleep after a particularly insightful or powerful journey, or conversely, that you have had a very hard time staying awake. Our bodies are telling us such an important story, and we really do need to listen to that wise inner voice.

This inner work can be exhausting and draining, or exhilarating and revitalizing. Whichever scenario plays out for you, remember that we definitely need to balance out the learnings and insights with taking a pause to reflect and integrate what we are learning. Without looking inward and reflecting, we do not renew ourselves.

Do you tend to deflect the insights that you are having, get busy in your "real life" and let your attention drop away from your importance and preciousness and what you are learning about yourself? Do you withdraw and resist applying the guidance that you have been offered by your higher self and your spirit helpers, by closing the doors and windows to your heart?

Check in to how you are feeling in your body. Are you present? Tired? Bored? Feeling stubborn toward change? Do you feel stupid or self-judgmental? Do you wonder if you should be further along the path than you feel you are right now? These might be indicators that you are out of balance in your personal work, and need to find some time to deepen your understanding, reflect on your progress so far, and give yourself a little pat on the back. Remember, that according to Christianity, even God took a day off from creating the world!

I recall a time in the not too distant past when I was running on empty. I was seeing a lot of clients, traveling quite a bit, and my father had some health issues. I was doing some of my inner work, but not balancing with time for integration, or being open to support from my Guidance or anyone else for that matter. I told myself that I am a healer, and should be able to help myself.

I was journeying one evening, and I was intent on taking this journey to relax. Not many moments after I began drumming, my Spirit Helpers showed me a picture of myself, on an operating table, with many of my friends around me cutting and pasting my body like pieces of a puzzle. I noticed that they were laughing and having such fun as they put my body parts back together in this virtual operating room. I asked my guides why they showed me this picture. What was the message? I implored them to give me the message in a way that I could understand.

They told me that I wasn't asking for help. I wasn't open to receiving the help of my friends or family. I did not heed their advice, and within a couple of days, my back was so sore I could barely walk, never mind see clients or make the drive into the city to visit my dad. I was flattened by my own stubbornness to ask for help.

As I lay in bed, unable to get up, I suddenly heard the voices of my spirit helpers and clearly saw the picture of me on the operating table again, this time, from the perspective of my being on that bed. I journeyed as I lay there, and opened to hearing the advice of my Guidance: "Call for a healer, healer!" They smiled as they said this.

I finally heeded their advice. I called a friend who is a brilliant healer, and she came over to help me. As she worked on me on all levels; physical, emotional, and spiritual, she coaxed me back into an understanding of the balance that I needed to bring back into my life once again. I was able to see things from the perspective of nurturing myself, and looking after the healer inside me, by asking for the support that I needed.

How do you reflect and notice where you are, if you are in balance, or what you might need to do for yourself to bring balance and reflection into your life, for rejuvenating and revitalizing your energy?

I suggest that, if you have been keeping a journeying diary or notebook, set aside a good long day or weekend to reread it. Take some special time to go over your journals, with the intention to allow balance, integration and processing into your life. Take stock of where you began your work and the insights that you have had over the time that you have been journeying. Notice any patterns. Observe without judgment as you read the healing story that you are writing for yourself.

I offer this beautiful healing ceremony as a gift you can give to yourself. Take as much time as you can; a Friday night, a weekend, a week, or even longer if you need to. Reflect on where you were when you started this work, where you have had the courage to allow yourself to go, and where you are today. Allow your Guidance to support you. You can still journey, and perform your daily practice, but the intention is for reflection and integration: renewing your energy, and regrouping if necessary. Acknowledging and appreciating yourself as you create with balance, honors your precious self. It isn't all about work, work, work. It isn't even about play, play, play. It is about bringing your deep and precious energy into balance in all aspects of your life.

Your personal reflection and rejuvenation ceremony may occur at a similar time each month, season, or year. I typically do most of my rebalancing work and renewal of my energy in the winter. I am like a hibernating bear, doing my inner work with reflection and deepening my understanding. My healing practice tends to be fairly steady and predictable over the winter, with a more consistent number of clients per week than at other times of the year. Client sessions are usually indoors, so there is less preparation time required for the setting up the tipi and fires for ceremony outside and the like. We have long nights and short days in the winter here, so I don't tend to be outdoors as long as I might be in other seasons.

This is the perfect time for me to recharge and reflect on my own growth. I also do other integration ceremonies throughout the year, but not usually for extended periods, as I might do in the winter. Energetically, I feel supported by the lessened hours of daylight and colder temperatures for the increased time to work with and for myself.

For your personal ceremony, set aside a special time that is just for you, and be sure that you will be able to focus on *you*. If you have chosen a day to do this reflective work, make it a day that you will not be disturbed. Don't plan to do much the evening before, or the day after. Really gift yourself with time for you. If you have small children or privacy is in short supply, use your imagination. Bathrooms are awesome spaces for ceremony, and usually the door locks. I realize that you cannot be in there for days on end, but you could possibly afford yourself an hour a night, for a week, or something like that.

Open sacred space. Set the intention to open to what is restorative for you at this particular moment. Ask your Guidance what is the most appropriate way to reflect and integrate the work that you have done. Ask them for your own personal prescription to administer this very important gift to yourself. As you begin to drum or listen to a drumming CD or transformative music, let yourself go to whatever Guidance you are drawn to and set the intention again. Keep in mind and in your consciousness that this prescription, this celebration that your guides are going to help you create, is especially for you. It is the mark of an initiation, a rite of passage, and an honoring of the journey that you have made thus far. You are invoking the equivalent of a vision quest to be facilitated by and for yourself, and you love and cherish yourself enough to be open to what your Guidance prescribes for you to do.

They may offer many ideas and images, and, as always, notice what you are feeling in your body.

My guides and teachers have given me many ideas for self-celebration. This is a wonderful reminder of your wholeness. Sometimes, Guidance will direct me to make something physical to represent my growth. Sometimes, they will suggest a specific activity, or a particular meditation with a certain theme.

I have journeyed on behalf of my regular clients for a celebration of wholeness, and a way to bring balance in their lives. Once, a client was instructed to make a beautiful mask, which was the representation of the beauty she was creating within herself. This wonderful mask is a focal point in her office, and it is a beautiful creation. She spent many enjoyable hours in the craft store picking brightly colored feathers and decorations for the mask. The day that was spent in actually creating the mask was filled with creative self-expression and a sense of empowerment.

Others have been instructed to take a trip out to the mountains to look for a certain item. I have been instructed by my guides to tell them to go for walks to search for feathers or flowers. Others have been told to construct a rattle or to take a drumming class. Some prescriptions offered by Guidance have been as simple as putting a bowl of lavender flowers in the bedroom, and smelling their beautiful fragrance. Your guides will tailor your special ceremony just for you.

I also encourage you to continue writing in your diary or your journal, and once renewed and rebalanced, consider the following journey to reclaim yourself in your balance, wisdom and renewed wholeness. Once you have opened sacred space, set the intention to honor your renewed energy, now rebalanced. From this sense of wholeness and revitalization, accept who you are in this moment, and who you will continue to become as you deepen into more truth and beauty, realizing your highest and most precious self.

Notice how you feel, listen to what your Guides tell you and honor the process that you are going through!

Chapter Fifteen

Working With Others – or –
Call Roadside Assistance

The effects of taking care of you in a loving way are amazing. Doing your inner work regularly is perhaps the biggest gift that you can offer yourself. Are you enjoying your journeying and having fun creating celebrations that reconnect you to the natural world? I am very sure that some profound insights have emerged from your travels, and that you are learning a lot about yourself.

Whether your friends are noticing changes in you or if you are attracting new friends, one thing is for certain: you will begin to realize that we are all connected energetically. We are all more similar than we are different!

If you have had the opportunity to host or attend a group celebration, or healing circle, listen carefully to what is shared, and, most importantly, feel what is going on inside you. So many people will share similar visions or experiences. Many will have similar reactions to the same triggers, positive or negative. Feel the energy in the room and how it feels in your body to be with like-minded people.

If participating in journeying circles, listen carefully to what people share when they are journeying with the same intention. The synergies and similarities in what people see, or the messages that they receive, often contain surprisingly similar threads running through them. The energy in a group will frequently intensify these threads, and when others share, it may bring more clarity to your own journey.

Some people may have problems learning to journey or to access their Guidance. Because you have had some experience with this now, perhaps you could assist them? Remember that the energetic power that the two of you are emanating is much more than twice that of one person. You can support another person and help them in ways that will really support their growth. This is friendship on a whole new level.

This is very intimate work, as you will be connecting energetically to another human being, and accessing personal, deep and potent information about them. It is not intimacy of a sexual nature, but certainly an experience that offers some intensity! Obviously, you must be prepared for the depth that your support may be received, and you must have absolutely *no* attachment to the outcome. You are not fixing or healing this person. You are supporting them on their spiritual journey.

Imagine holding your arms out in front of you and coaxing the person to gently step forward into their true loving nature. In no way should they be pushed or shoved into anything! This is sacred work, and must be held in respect, reverence and deep compassion. The most important part of assisting others is that the person must give you *permission* to help them. You cannot journey on someone's behalf without their knowledge or expressed approval. This would be an invasion of their privacy, and is not ethical in the shamanic world.

Another very important reminder is that you are an equal. If you have offered your assistance to another, and they have given you permission to help them, you are in no way superior to them. You have just achieved a level of understanding that allows you to be of support and service to another.

I learned this very lesson during a session in my healing practice. When I work with clients, I often have insights into their issues and how they have manifested dis-ease in their body. My guides are showing me lots of things to assist me with my work, as always. During one particularly busy and challenging week, I was working intently with one person.

I "knew" what was happening for her, and although I felt I was gently facilitating in guiding her toward some insights about herself, I suddenly heard a voice in my head. It was like a little child, goading someone, saying, "I know something you don't know!" I'm not proud of the words I heard, or the thoughts that I was having in that moment. I instantly felt the pain that was rising from my solar plexus toward my heart. I knew in that moment that I was feeling superior. I felt superior to this client, and deep down, I knew that energetically that was not the truth and it was certainly not appropriate in my capacity as her healer!

I had the presence to excuse myself, and interrupt what she was saying to share with her what was happening for me. I shared with her what I was feeling in my body. I shared the thoughts that were running through my head. I needed to remain in my body, and look at what was going on for me in that moment. I realized that I was not doing my best work for this person, as I was not in my own wholeness in the moment. I told her that it was my intention to do my best to be of service and support her, as I healed what was happening in me.

I was able to take a few minutes, recognize what was going on for me, and reconnect with my Guidance. I felt the pain in my solar plexus and heart and set the intention to heal what was going on within me. I sensed that this was the opposite to what I can usually feel about myself, which is inferior, but the Universe was reminding me that I was simply not feeling equal. I re-established my grounding, and with a clear intention of compassion and equality for my client, and myself, I was able to continue with the session.

I told my client that I had been out of my integrity in that moment. I asked her to accept my apology, and that my intention was to be compassionate with her, and from a place of equality, shared the healing story with her. The healing story was how I was able to bring myself into a state of equality, and remind myself of my wholeness. Only in that state of wholeness could I support her, and not allow my fear, which manifested as a sense of superiority, to be in control of the session. The experience that happened in that moment was healing for both of us. I was able to see, feel and know my equality in the moment.

My client said I had demonstrated to her how she could challenge her fears and be in her own wholeness. She appreciated my willingness to be vulnerable, and knew that she would be able to consider experimenting with feeling vulnerable herself. It was a profound way to learn together!

When a friend or a colleague opens up to you and you feel that you can support them, open a dialogue for sharing and do your best to be in your wholeness, or to be aware of when you may not be.

You are stepping into a somewhat different role in your life now. What do you notice as you are considering helping someone else as they move onto their healing path? Can you be clear that you are being of service from a true sense of equality and compassion? Are you willing to be open and vulnerable when you may fall out of your integrity in a moment, as I did in that important client session? Can you be that honest with yourself and the person that you are with? These are always the important aspects of challenging fear... the willingness to explore the depths of your willingness to be honest, vulnerable and compassionate.

At this stage of your personal growth, I suggest that you journey for another in a capacity that will be empowering for both of you. The first partner journey that I teach in groups is to journey to connect your partner with a power animal or helper.

In a group setting, or while working with a partner, set the intention to support, and journey to Non-Ordinary Reality to meet a power animal or helping spirit who will be of assistance to your partner at this time. They may already have and work with a powerful helping spirit, but please know that we can all have more than one, and that each of our helping spirits may offer help and support in different ways.

Sit beside your partner as you set this intention. Have them lie or sit comfortably, as you open space, smudge with them, and set intentions. When I am journeying for someone else, I state in the intention that I am journeying on behalf of someone else. Then, begin your journey on their behalf, to retrieve a helping spirit. Drum for yourself, or play the CD of drumming music that you resonate with.

Just as in your own journeys, you will be drawn to Non-Ordinary Reality. Remember, if you get "lost" what your purpose is. Restate your intention. When you meet animals or helping spirits, ask them if they are for your friend, and wait for the answer. You are practiced now at journeying, and recognize that you can converse with whomever you meet. Ask the power animal or teacher if they have a message for your friend, and listen carefully to the response.

Share with your partner who you met, and express the message that was to be passed on – if the helping spirit offered one. It is fine if they didn't offer anything directly to you. Your friend can now make the choice to deepen his or her relationship with the entity that you have introduced. Also, do not be surprised if it is not a power animal that returns. It could be a healing spirit of any type, which needs to be brought back to help this person at this time. You may not be drawn to the Lower World. You may have a journey of a completely different type. Don't be afraid to share what is returned. Whatever happened is for your partner, and not you.

I recently held a workshop where people were learning to perform divination journeys for others, of which a power animal retrieval journey is an example. One participant felt very embarrassed when we were sharing what happened during their journey for their partner. She had retrieved a fairy like creature for her partner. She was so worried that she had done the journey incorrectly. The partner, on the other hand, was deeply moved by the return of this childhood friend, now reconnected and remembered, and it was a very healing experience!

In another deeper healing journey, the practitioner brings the *essence* of the animal back to the client. It is brought back from Non-Ordinary Reality in a variety of creative ways, according to the guidance given to the practitioner: some carry the helper back in their hands, or in a crystal used for this purpose, for example. Whatever the method of transportation, this beautiful helping spirit is then blown into the heart and crown of the recipient in a loving a compassionate way, offering healing to the client. The client then imagines, feels and knows that this helping spirit is being absorbed into every cell of their bodies using a predetermined metaphor of absorption.

I am constantly amazed by the coincidences or synchronicities that are shared by the person when their power is restored to them. They will share that they had a particular affinity with their animal as a child, for example, a favorite stuffed bear or monkey, or a collection of ceramic horses or wolves. Many have experienced visions or dreams containing the particular form of power that was retrieved for them at the same time that the journey on their behalf was happening. When I have blown the power animal or spirit form into their body, they have described it to me, before I have had a chance to tell them what it was that was returned or newly joined them.

The results of a restoration of power are inspiring. I have had clients remind me about the way they felt having a treasured teddy bear in tow: safe, comforted and strong. They resonate with the attributes of the animal or guardian that has been brought back. Generally, a sense of revitalized energy is restored, and the client is then ready to continue on their healing path with more vitality and verve.

My experience with this restoration of power is that the person should then be encouraged to take on a regular practice of inner work, meditation or journeying to integrate, understand, and continually empower themselves with deepening connections with their guardian spirits.

As their friend, I would offer elements of your practice as an example, allowing them to modify it for their own intentions, purpose and resonance. This is a perfect time for them to dance their power animal, merging with this returned energy and essence. Encourage them to continue their integration with this Spirit Helper. They can dance on their own, or with you or a group, if you are working in a healing circle. Please be sure to remind them that their newly reconnected Helping Spirit does not possess them or is in any way taking them over, and they are always in control. Remember that you are assisting this other person, and because you know how to journey, and have been practicing, you are offering your support. In no way are you superior or "better" than them. Be sure to check your ego at the door.

If you are looking now to share this work to more deeply assist others in their healing, remembering that this deepens your own work, then it is appropriate to offer more guidance to support your community. You must always continue to do your own work, remember your own wholeness, and explore these deeper shamanic practices if you are honestly feeling called to it. This work is powerful and effective, and cannot be minimized. You should be more than just curious about working with others, and should feel called to follow this extraordinary path of healing.

In the following section, stay present in your body, and note if any of these symptoms are your own. Consider if you should be seeking a practitioner for yourself, to heal wounds within yourself. It is also profound to experience the work of a shamanic practitioner before you attempt to help others.

You must also be aware of the causes of illness in yourself and others. From a shamanic perspective, there are three causes for illness or dis-ease. These three root causes of disease are *power loss* – a disconnection from the empowering spiritual allies that walk with us, *soul loss* – where a part of our soul essence has "left" this state of reality due to trauma, as a means of protecting the psyche, or a *spiritual intrusion* – where an intrusive spirit or element is misplaced within a person. Each type of "illness" presents itself somewhat differently in terms of symptoms.

A person suffering from *power loss* typically presents depression, constant illness or chronic misfortune, for example, in a series of accidents. The client feels low in energy and disconnected from friends, loved ones and community. If your friend is exhibiting these symptoms, then it is possible that they would require a power animal retrieval, one of the most common early journeys to assist another shamanically. It is the next step to the power animal journey shared with you earlier in this chapter.

After their permission is granted, set up a time that is appropriate for both of you, when you will not be disturbed and you can be relaxed together. Your role as the practitioner is to journey on behalf of your friend, to retrieve a power animal that they may have become disconnected with, and is willing to return to assist them now.

Prepare your friend for what you will be doing. Explain to them that you will be drumming and rattling, and that you are entering a kind of trance, so that you can enter another reality to retrieve a power animal for them. Once you stop drumming, you will be blowing the essence of whatever you retrieve into their heart and their crown chakra and that once you do, their job is to absorb the essence of this helping spirit into their body fully.

Before the journey begins, discuss with them their need for a metaphor to absorb this energy into them. Great metaphors for absorption include images such as pouring water on dry sand, and seeing the water spread through the dry earth. Maybe they could relate to watering a wilting flower and seeing it revive, or seeing a sponge sucking up water off the floor: anything that feels to them like they would be engaged in the absorption of the returned energy completely and thoroughly.

As always, since this is a ceremony for healing, you must do your utmost to be in your integrity, in other words, in your wholeness. Open sacred space. Be clear on your intention, and state this to your guides and teachers. You are traveling to Non-Ordinary Reality on behalf of (*state your friend's name*) to retrieve an animal spirit helper that is ready to come to assist (*state the name*) at this time.

Lay down next to your friend, touching at the shoulders, hips and ankles if possible, if they are comfortable with that, and start the drumming CD. If you drum for yourself, sit up with your knee touching them, again as long as they are comfortable with your touching them. Travel with your power animal to the Lower World, or wherever your helping spirits take you.

Remembering your intention, look around Non-Ordinary Reality for the spirit animal for your friend. Ask animals that you come across on your journey whether they are for your friend, and whether they are willing to come back at this time to help. When you find the one that is for your friend, in your imagination, hold out your hands, palms up, and let the animal come into your hands. I envision holding the essence of this animal close to my heart. When the drumming plays the call back, or you stop drumming, bring yourself fully back into your physical body gently. Kneel beside your friend and, in ordinary reality, hold out your hands, with the essence of their power animal in it, and place your cupped hands over their heart. Bend down and blow the essence into their heart. Move to the top of their head and blow into the crown chakra at the top of their head. As long as they have a healthy back, you can assist them in sitting up for you to blow the essence into the crown. If they cannot sit up, have them continue to lie down, as you maneuver yourself to be able to blow the essence into the crown. Gently remind them to begin their metaphor for absorption now. I rattle in a large circle encompassing their heart and head at least four times. This "seals in" the essence.

Tell your friend that they need not rush back... to take the time that they need to deeply feel the return of the Spirit Helper. This is when they are going to be using their metaphor of absorbing the essence fully into their being. While they are integrating the essence, I will wait patiently, or jot down a few notes to share with them. It is important for you as the practitioner to be supportive energetically as they absorb this energy. Please stay quietly with them as you write or just sit. It is also a powerful experience to transfigure as the client is absorbing the energy.

The story that you can share with them when they are ready is a healing story. Tell them a bit about how and where you found their power animal, and if it shared any messages with you about how excited it is to return. If you found any information out about what qualities this animal has come back to offer, that would be helpful, but if you didn't get anything, please don't speculate. Let the newly reunited host and their spirit animal be with their insights and truth for themselves.

If you saw anything traumatic, like the cause of the spirit animal disconnecting, please do not remind the person of this. Do not tell them things that are not healing. What would be your intention for doing that? They do not need reminding of a painful situation now that their reconnection has been made with their loving spirit companion! That deeper work may have to be done later, but it does not have to happen now. Merely share the healing aspects of the reuniting of these compassionate spirits. Take great care on your part to share the wonderful healing aspects of the return of power to your friend as this is your responsibility and your gift as a healing practitioner.

The client who is suffering *soul loss* continually looks outside of himself to feel complete. We suffer psychological trauma in many instances in this modern world, and when we experience such trauma, sometimes, the psyche cannot handle the pain. Shamanically speaking; a part of our essence leaves this reality, projecting itself into another reality. For those who have suffered major trauma such as an automobile accident, physical or psychological abuse, divorce, or death of a loved one, the traumatic incident causing the soul loss can be obvious, but there are others that are less obvious, but equally as painful. An incident of ridicule on the job, or in school, being the recipient of an act of road rage, or watching a TV program that affects us deeply may seem insignificant at the time, but may create tremendous soul loss. Whatever the cause – and there are many – the symptoms of soul loss are: separation from the event itself, dissociation from self and others, feeling disconnected and not in the body, constant illness, depression, addiction(s) and a general feeling of weakness, feeling fragmented or powerlessness.

Victims of soul loss sometimes suffer lapses of memory, which may include blocking out the memory of the traumatic event itself. Soul loss through the loss of a loved one may present as endless and unrelenting grief. The sufferer will often use words such as, "I have never been the same since...." or, "I just can't seem to let go of this." The soul loss sufferer searches for something to fill the void that their missing essence is creating.

Until you are really well versed and comfortable with supporting others, and have had some expert training in the area of soul retrieval, I would not suggest that you perform soul retrieval on anyone. This is not a particularly easy or well-advised journey to do on yourself, either. If you feel that you or someone you know has suffered soul loss, please contact a shamanic practitioner to perform the soul retrieval. If you resonate very strongly with doing this type of work, and wish to be of service to others, contact a shamanic teacher to instruct you in how to do this wonderful and meaningful work.

The effects of soul retrievals are as varied as the people who receive it. With many, there is some sort of change experienced, described as a feeling of "lightness" or that they feel "full". Some clients have mentioned that colors are brighter, and that their senses seemed heightened. They feel more in tune with their bodies. Some people do feel disoriented. They have received soul parts back that will make significant changes in their vibrational energy, and this requires integration.

A myriad of emotions have come up during soul retrieval sessions: laughter, tears and memories of an incident previously forgotten that may surprise or upset them. There is no way of predicting these results. As the practitioner, always wait for the client to share their experience. A significant traumatic event suffered as a child is often much different when seen from the perspective of an adult, so even with abuse sufferers, one can never predict the reactions from a returned soul part. Effects can even be delayed, not surfacing for several hours, days or weeks. Soul retrieval is not an end, but a new beginning, with new awareness and a renewed sense of wholeness. That can take some getting used to, but it also marks an important juncture in a client's healing.

There can be an overlapping of symptoms, and what is therefore retrieved for the client. A power animal or helping spirit might be willing to return to the client who has suffered soul loss, as this soul loss has also resulted in power loss. Integration of the soul part may require the return of this powerful aspect and, if so, the practitioner will be guided to return this essence as well. A diagnostic journey is generally the best place to start, to gain clarity on what is required for the best healing for the client.

If you suspect or are noticing an overlap of symptoms, again, please look for a practitioner to perform the work, or get the necessary training. If your friend is open, and the practitioner is used to working in a group setting, it is very supportive to have a friend present when receiving these powerful healings. This is also a beautiful creation of community with loving energetic assistance.

The other type of illness that shamanic practitioners recognize is the *spiritual intrusion*. The shamanic definition of an intrusion is that *misplaced* energy enters a body that is experiencing an emotional and energetic void caused by, for example, soul loss.

This state of being opens up the energetic body to intrusions, which are able to "invade" or enter the host. Intrusions present as localized pain, or an old injury that doesn't go away. Chronic fatigue is often an indicator of an intrusion. This work is powerful and effective for the sufferer, but it is very important that the practitioner be very clear on their own boundaries and safety, as an intrusion may leave the current host, and latch onto the practitioner if care is not taken. This is precisely why this type of work requires training from an experienced teacher.

Our stressful, busy world offers many opportunities for spiritual intrusion. For example, if I am feeling angry or jealous of a particular person, and do not express these feeling in a healthy way, I may inadvertently send an intrusion to that person. Intrusions are energetic, and in a crowded city, with many people engaged in their traumas and dramas, one can only imagine the streams of psychic "darts" and "bullets" that might be flying around!

It is important to note that these intrusions are *not evil*, but merely *misplaced*. They have found a nice place to be in their new host, and do not necessarily know that there is somewhere else they should or could be. There is even a distinction between energetic intrusions, requiring extraction, and conscious beings with a soul that have possessed a subject, requiring depossession. Again, these are not evil, but simply lost souls who require a shamanic practitioner to perform psychopomp work on them, to show the possessing lost spirit the way home.

It is not suggested that you perform extraction work without proper instruction or support from a practitioner or teacher. Please be very careful, as these are situations where you could pick up a displaced spirit when it is removed from someone, if you are not very aware of and confident in what you are doing.

You are always "safe" and doing great work when you perform healings while being in your most radiant light, created in a wonderful state of transfiguration as you radiate! This is healing for any "ill". Remember that you are not directing your light at anyone or anything, but merely being in a state of Divine Light and energy. You can never hurt anyone as you work in this way.

If in doubt, sit with your friend in need, and transfigure. This is one of the safest, and most supportive things that we can do for others, the planet and ourselves! Remember that you are radiant light. You view your friend in their radiant perfection, whole in every way. Be in your light, luminous and loving. You do not direct your light towards them. Just be your luminous spiritual light. This is a most loving, compassionate way to heal.

Remember the cardinal rule: do no harm. What I take from this statement is to be in your most whole state with a very clear intention. Have respect and reverence for the work. Understand your level of comfort and the knowledge that you have around the healing work that you might be undertaking. Please take instruction for the work that is most intimate and complex, and could possibly hamper the well-being of not only your client but yourself as well. There is no such thing as being too cautious. This is powerful and impactful work.

Our biggest gift is to be our most radiant, compassionate, luminous selves, as we create in love. To share this light in the creation of the new dream is our greatest contribution.

Chapter Sixteen

Working With Children – or – Are We There Yet? Are We There Yet?

What a wonderful opportunity our new dream can hold for our children! What would the world look like if we nurtured their imaginations and honored the important transitions that they go through in their lives as they grow and learn?

I love to work with young children, as they have not yet lost their connection with Source energy or with the magic that is in their imagination. They love to rattle and drum, and I feel that this is an important way to stay connected to their helping spirits.

Kids will often speak about their invisible friends, and will tell you tons of stories about the antics that they get up to with these fantastic companions. As parents or grandparents, we often quell these stories, asking the child to be quiet, as the stories embarrass us in front of our friends or relatives. I encourage and nurture the child to believe in the magic, even though I am careful to tell them that they might not want to share this with everyone; maybe just family for now. Not that it is a secret, or something bad, or something to be discouraged, but to keep the story special and sacred.... which to me means sharing it with people you love and who love you. It would never be my intention to set up a child to be bullied by someone who is not understanding of the deep and powerful meanings of these stories.

We also need to be diligent if a child were to share something that is clearly violent or self-harming, or self-deprecating, and support them in recognizing that. Clearly, there are healthy boundaries to be maintained as we nurture and support our little ones.

It is fun and enjoyable to listen attentively and respectfully to a child's stories of magic, or to listen to them recount their dreams and what they are excited about. Kids are so much closer to remembering their spiritual light, and they love to transfigure, as I mentioned early in the book. I have led circles of children in dancing in their radiance, and it is so astounding to watch them dancing and radiating such beautiful light. They literally light up the room!

Kids have a lot of milestones throughout their young lives, and then into their teen years. I encourage you to honor their important dates. Of course, there is their special day – their birthday. Not only can you celebrate with a cake and friends over for a party, but you might share with them the story of their birth. This is a common practice in some native cultures where the extraordinary story of the birth of the child is retold every year. It is a lovely way to remember their entrance to the Earth School, and it is also a lovely time for the parents and child to be together in deep bonding.

We celebrate some major birthdays in a more lavish style than others, for example sweet sixteen or the entry into adulthood at eighteen or twenty-one. These are great times for a very loving celebration of their lives thus far.

Physical changes in their bodies can also be celebrated. The magic of the tooth fairy is one story that, for me, never loses its enchantment. I also think it is lovely to keep these tiny teeth to give back to the child later in life. If they wish to follow a medicine or shamanic path, these precious items are placed in their medicine bags as signs of power, transition, initiation and openness to change.

Although it is not so widespread within our own Western culture, there are many places around the world that celebrate a young person's transition into puberty. Let your Guidance show you the way for what might be your family's way to honor this important shift of energy in your young person's life.

It is honoring and respectful to revere these changes in our children's life, and to celebrate the people they are becoming.

How better to have a deep knowledge of who your child really is, so that if, for whatever reason, they stray from their path, you can not only notice sooner, and maybe be of more assistance, but also support them in a more nurturing, healthy and respectful way?

I have friends in the shamanic community that share stories from their children. The knowledge and wisdom that a child possesses is magnificently connected to a divine truth, and fills me with inspiration and hopefulness.

In nurturing our young ones, it comes to mind that these youngsters of today will be the ones looking after us in the latter parts of our lives. I firmly believe we will get back what we have given to our future caregivers! My intention is to nurture them with love so that they have the opportunity to reach their potential on the Earth School. Of course, we don't know what the Universe has in store for them, nor do we know what they came into this life to learn. Let's allow them the freedom of choosing what they need to learn from these lessons in their own best way.

The great gift we offer our children is our legacy. Perhaps if we thought of that aspect from the day they were born, rather than when we are getting old, we would nurture and raise them differently. How do we want to be remembered?

I was not following a shamanic path when our daughter was born. I came to this information later in my life, when she was about sixteen. We had some tumultuous times, when I was trying to control and manipulate her into doing what I thought was best for her. She, of course, resisted that fear-based parenting.

Since I have been learning more about myself, and have shared my fears and joys with her as I have gained awareness around them, we have changed our relationship dramatically. Nothing fills my heart so much as when we have participated in ceremonies together. I was proud to have her attend my adoption and naming ceremony into my Native American family. Because she is my daughter, she is also a member of this adopted family.

She seems to have an openness and acceptance of people

without judgment, and it is my hope that this is a legacy that I have passed onto her. She is a lovely young woman, living in her authenticity with an amazing amount of wisdom. I feel blessed to be watching her grow.

These young people are our future. When I have journeyed to the descendants, I see a possible future that is bright, hopeful and serene. It is filled with light. I believe that is because we are having glimpses of this dream, and starting to create it with our children.

Chapter Seventeen

The Future is Yours – or – What Is On The Road Ahead?

You are never alone. Your own personal team of helping spirits, who sincerely wish only love for you, guide you. Your love is the fuel for their existence. Your shamanic journeys can take you into realms of existence that you never thought possible. These quests take you to your own personal truth and ignite you from the inside out, compelling you to be your most radiant light. In radiant energy, all healing is possible.

Your guides hold a guiding light that illuminates your path – your path, and no one else's. They show you the way ahead, with lots of signposts along the way. If you get lost, they will help you find your direction again, and set you back on a healing path, reminding you about your choices, if you choose to listen to their wise words.

It is your responsibility to listen, choose, and then take action. No one makes your life happen for you. You are creating your own experiences. You are doubtlessly getting that message if you are taking heed of your spiritual helpers, as you do your inner work. Through images, sounds, feelings or a sense of inner knowing, only you can choose to empower yourself, or continue on a path that is fueled by fear. How will you choose?

Will you share your journey by creating a community? We all need a tribe or companions who will support us truthfully and honestly. How can we learn to interact with the deepest parts of ourselves, communicate with our Spirit Helpers, and be in relationship with others so that we learn the truth about ourselves and the potential that each of us holds as an individual?

We are in an amazing time of human evolution. We have been

given an opportunity by the Universe to press a restart button – that is to create with love and compassion the way that we mean to go on. We are being shown that we have choice, and that there is no need to consider that we should suffer: each lesson, each circumstance is an opportunity for growth. When looked at in that way, events are not "sad" or "tragic", but a joyful opportunity to grow and learn.

This concept of suffering has been thematic in my practice. Most clients have been entering the session feeling like victims to their circumstances, but after discussion and opening to Guidance, they are seeing and experiencing the wisdom of the opportunity being offered to them by the Universe. What is equally important is that they are being offered the physical experience within their body. In other words, they are sensing the difference of being a victim, or an empowered co-creator in their lives, by *feeling* the physical sensations of their choice of perspectives.

We are becoming more connected through our inner universe – the experience of being here at this time and place is a sensory one, and more and more of us gather in community to experience these sensations and share with compassion and honesty. We are becoming more open to discussing how we are feeling – and that these discussions are healings in their own right. This is a time of feeling equal with one another, as we experience the true nature of our spirits and souls together. As we reconnect to nature and all its aspects, we are healthier, happier and filled with more joy.

My life has been enriched by the shamanic practices that I have shared with you throughout these pages. I continue to challenge my own fears of inadequacy and unworthiness, as they never seem to completely disappear in me. They might be lurking at a deeper level and, when unearthed, I continue to challenge them in the best way that I know how: I embrace the light of who I am, and refuse to let these fears limit me. I do not allow the fear to control my life and make my world small.

I sincerely intend to create through the expansion of love in my heart. I create ceremony and ritual in my life to do my best to make my whole life the meditation that it is meant to be. I perceive and feel peace in my life, and for many, many moments during my day, I feel empowered and radiant as I consider my own beautiful light.

My goal is always to create freedom in my life. Freedom for me is peace, tranquility, empowerment, self-love and being in service with compassion. Anything that does not contribute to that intention, I choose not to engage in. In the moments that I forget or lose sight of what is taking me on the road to this freedom, or if I am creating in a fearful way, I intend to choose from the most loving and peaceful part of me as soon as and as best as I can. Each time I choose from fear, I intend to learn more about myself, not from a judgmental place, but as a loving observer.

Journeying, ritual, and ceremony help me be the observer in my own life. Together with my Guidance, I explore what is happening for me in my life. I have learned to be more objective and less self-judgmental. I see myself from the viewpoint of my Spirit Helpers, who are allowing me to shift into my highest potential.

This work can be done anywhere. You have been offered ceremonies, rituals and meditations that you can even do in your office at work. You do not need to travel to an ashram and converse with a guru. Everything you hold onto here in your hometown you will take with you to the ashram, good or bad. What you learn in the ashram may not translate well into your daily life, if you have no tools for integration of these learnings. You will not find anything outside yourself that will serve to value you or make you feel better in the long run. The answer is inside you. All your answers lie within.

With reverence for your own life, you create reverence for all things. With love for yourself, you create more love in the world.

With gratitude for the abundance that you have in your life, you create more abundance. Ask your Spirit Helpers and they will show you how!

The cycles of your life will continue to deepen as you deepen your self-exploration. The circles will bring in more meaning and information as you have courage to ask the tough questions and wait for the tougher answers. Then do more work. And then do some more.

Don't forget to invite balance and time for processing and integration. That is part of the cycle, too. Once renewed, then open to deepening understanding and insight. Once deepened, allow integration. Integrate and apply what you are learning into your daily life. Then renew again.

Helpers surround you. You are never alone!

Chapter Eighteen

Additional Resources – or – Your Vehicle's Owner's Manuals

Because your life's work and your ongoing self-exploration require you to have awareness and presence, one of the greatest gifts you can give yourself is emotional awareness. This awareness has been a brilliant foundation for the inner work that I have done for myself and continue to do to the best of my ability in every moment.

To gain insight into the feelings in my physical body, and their meaning – the messages from my soul, I was fortunate to have as my teachers and mentors, Gary Zukav and Linda Francis. I experienced many very painful years as I explored, but with their brilliant counsel and direction, I learned vital information about myself. I gained awareness about the fear-based parts of my personality that were limiting my life. I was encouraged in how to challenge these frightened parts of my personality and choose differently. I realized that it was more painful to remain as I was, creating from the fearful parts of my personality, than it was to experience painful messages from my soul, with the intention to heal. Their website is www.seatofthesoul.com and I strongly encourage you to explore this work.

Shamanism came into my life initially through the brilliant book *Soul Retrieval* by Sandra Ingerman. She is, in my mind, the leading authority on bringing shamanism into the modern world. She is a gifted writer, facilitator, shamanic practitioner, teacher and mentor. I have not experienced a more supportive and generous teacher, who truly wants this work to be brought into the world, to effect global and planetary healing. Sandra's website is www.sandraingerman.com. She is a prolific writer, with many books and CDs available, and even has an app for the iPhone and iPad! Shamanism is really entering the twenty-first century. She also holds workshops that are an absolute joy to attend. She is supportive of all the practitioners and teachers that she trains, and lists them on www.shamanicteachers.com and on her website, should you be interested in finding a practitioner or teacher near where you live. Sandra's website also offers links to the Society of Shamanic Practitioners, an alliance of persons committed to shamanic practices.

The person credited for bringing awareness to shamanism back into these times is Michael Harner. His book, *The Way of the Shaman*, is the foremost authority on the subject. Information on the Foundation for Shamanic Studies, which is his non-profit organization in support of preserving the study and teaching of shamanic wisdom, can be found at www.shamanism.org.

If you want to do more reading on spirit animals, I recommend books by Ted Andrews. *Animal-Speak* and *Nature-Speak* are perhaps the quintessential books for deepening understanding of animal and plant energy and behaviors.

Another very good book about spirit animals is Steven D. Farmer's book *Animal Spirit Guides*. I like it as it is very well laid out, easy to use, and very thorough. It is a very handy reference should you need deeper understanding of why an animal may have shown up for you in journeying.

There are some very good music CDs that I use during my work, if drumming for myself is not warranted or possible. One of the most transformational CDs that I recommend for transfiguration work is Wavepool, by Robert Rand. Other CDs I really like are Shamanic Healing, Whale Meditation and Quiet Earth all by Kamal. I also recommend CDs by Anugama. For a more indigenous theme with native drumming, I love David and Steve Gordon's work. They have several CDs including Sacred Drum Visions, which is beautiful.

For drumming CDs to be used specifically for journeying, Sandra Ingerman's book *Shamanic Journeying: A Beginner's Guide* includes a CD for this purpose. Tracks have the required call back and return beats.

Acknowledgements

I am very grateful for my life. I am blessed in so many ways. My loving husband, Mike, always supports me, and encourages me to push through any of the doubts I have about myself. I cannot imagine what the last thirty years would have been like without Mike's generous love, truth and incredible humor.

I am thankful for our beautiful daughter, Dyan, whose deep blue eyes express the expansiveness of her soul. She has taught me so much about compassion and love without judgment. I am so blessed that she is in my life!

My loving family: my mom, although not on the Earth School for many years, was always ahead of her time. She encouraged me to be an individual, and to have a strong sense of purpose. My dad reminds me daily of the strength and tenacity of my ancestors. My sister Maggie is an inspiring, positive force in my life, and I am grateful to have her by my side.

I have sisters who are not of my blood, but are sisters just the same. Marlene, Vicki, Laini, Gail, Janet, Patti, and Carol E, your supportive energy is always a loving reminder of the bond that I have with my dearest ones!

Adam and Pierre, you encouraged me to enter onto the path of a healer. Your inspiration changed my life. I have so much love for both of you!

I offer deep gratitude to my adopted Stoney brother, Roland. You encouraged me to share the wisdom that has been given to me from the Great Mother, and your stories about the ancestors remind me that we are connected by something much deeper than our blood. Your brilliant artwork is a tribute to the loving gift you have been given by the Creator, and your passion for life. You encouraged me to write again.

My clients, many of whom have become good friends have mirrored aspects of great learning for me. I am honored that I have been of service and in turn, have received so much.

I am so grateful for the teachers that I have had in my life. Gary and Linda, you have assisted me in ways that I cannot adequately express in words. You helped me to find my true voice.

All my fellow participants in the Authentic Power Program who shared of themselves so deeply; you offered me so much clarity of insight as I observed your growing and changing, so that I could have the courage to do the same in my own life. I hold so many of you close to my heart.

Sandra, you are a brilliant light, and encourage me and remind me of my own brilliant light, from your example. Your generosity and sharing is an inspiration! Your devotion to creating community is a blessing. I am so grateful that you are in my life.

To all of the participants in Sandra Ingerman's Teacher Training. I am inspired and in awe of the gifted group of people from all over the globe that I have drawn into my life. With such compassion and integrity, the work that all of us can do together creates the new dream!

MOON
BOOKS

Moon Books invites you to begin or deepen your encounter with Paganism, in all its rich, creative, flourishing forms.